LIFE TOUCHED WITH WONDER

LIFE TOUCHED WITH WONDER

The POWER *of* HEALING

FROM THE EDITORS OF READER'S DIGEST

THE READER'S DIGEST ASSOCIATION, INC.
PLEASANTVILLE, NEW YORK

CONTENTS

LIFE TOUCHED WITH WONDER

Men wonder at the height of mountains, the huge waves of the sea, the broad flow of rivers, the course of the stars—and forget to wonder at themselves.
— *St. Augustine*

We feel awe when we see a grand landscape or view the majesty of a starry sky. But there's also wonder in a child's kiss when you're feeling down, in a friend's unexpected recovery from a frightening illness, in a walk on a hushed, snowy night. Such moments take us by surprise and lift us from the mundane and the familiar. Suddenly, inexplicably, we catch a glimpse of a reality beyond ourselves, and see evidence that there is something beautiful, merciful, loving knit into the fabric of creation — even in ourselves.

In fact, ordinary people can be the most gifted messengers of wonder. Their stories offer compelling evidence of the power of the spirit in daily life. In this new book series we have selected the best of such true-life stories and present them in separate volumes organized around themes, including hope, love, courage and healing.

The Power of Healing is a collection of true stories showing how compassion as well as medicine, forgiveness as well as knowledge can renew lives. These stories will speak to the deepest level of your soul. They might even help heal the wounds in your own life.

THE DAY MY SILENT BROTHER SPOKE

BY
JIM WATSON

It was my mother's wedding day — a hot July morning in a small stone church in the foothills of Virginia's Blue Ridge Mountains. She was 60 and never more radiant as she opened this new chapter in her life. Outside the church, Mother called us together for a few serious words.

"Go see Grandma now," she said. "Don't be upset if she doesn't know you." Strokes and heart disease had left my 89-year-old grandmother lying crumpled and uncomprehending in a nursing-home bed.

As I drove through town, I looked around at my passengers. Here we were, the grandchildren: a banker, an entrepreneur, a musician, a lawyer, a journalist. And next to the window in the back seat, sitting quietly, was Page. How would this affect him? Probably not at all. He would never understand.

Page, my younger brother by four years, has been brain-damaged from birth. He does not speak, cannot hear and sees poorly through his remaining eye. He stopped growing when he was five feet tall and struggles against obesity. A wall of autism shuts him away from the outside world. He spends most of his time lost in his own musings, nodding, laughing, clucking and crying at a pageant only he can see.

Growing up, his brothers played football, drove cars, made friends and dated pretty girls. Page stayed home, entertaining himself on a rope swing, staring at television or playing with a flashlight — his lifelong fascination. One by one, the rest of us went off to school, got jobs, married and moved away. Page traveled to dreary institutions and rehabilitation centers, where he learned the basics of reading and using tools. Now 34, he has a room in a private home and a job with a small workshop for people like him. He is on his own, and at last he is happy. But it wasn't always this way.

During his teens, Page struggled with the emotional overload of adolescence. Seized by fits of anger, he would burst into uncontrollable tears, rake his fingernails down his face until his cheeks bled or, frustrated by newly forming cataracts, jab at his eyes with pencils. He passed through several distinct phases, each marked by a peculiar ritual.

First there was ground-kissing. Every so often, for no apparent reason, he would stop in midstep, drop to his knees and give the floor or sidewalk a long, passionate kiss. Wiping the dirt from his lips, he would calmly stand up and, with an air of accomplishment, continue on his way.

Ground-kissing gave way to spinning in place. From a sitting position, Page would suddenly stand up, twirl around as if he were unwinding himself from an invisible string and then, satisfied, take his seat. He whirled three times — never more, never less. One Sunday in church, Page decided to "unravel" during the sermon. First, a rustle of papers and clothes. Then he stood, knocking a hymnal loudly to the floor. All eyes turned to investigate the disturbance. Children gawked, bewildered. I stared at the church bulletin, my face burning.

For years, my reaction to Page's behavior was embarrassment, anger, resentment. *Why him? Why me?* I was sure he saved his most humiliating

stunts for when we were in public. People stared. Page was strange. Did they think there was something strange about our whole family — about me?

As I got older, however, I began to understand that he had no control over his actions, that I could not judge him as I judge others. He wasn't trying to be difficult or strange. He was simply lost, never to be found.

As he drifted further away, I gave up trying to recover the brother I had been denied. Shame and anger turned into acceptance. In time, if I caught anyone staring at the frowning, clucking little fat man with hearing aids in both ears and pockets bulging with flashlights and magnifying glasses, I stared back defiantly.

Just before we left for the nursing home, Mom had penciled the words "VISIT GRANDMA" for Page in large letters on a napkin. Yet no one expected him to grasp our purpose, to understand that this might be our last visit.

As I drove, other memories floated through my mind: memories of 80-year-old Grandma, arms like sticks, pushing her old power mower up the slope of her back yard, dismissing able-bodied volunteers with a shrug. Grandma's thin, shaking fingers carefully unwrapping Christmas presents to avoid tearing the paper, which she folded neatly by her side. And, of course, talking. Always talking.

The sound of Grandma's voice accompanies every memory of her. She spoke not in sentences or even paragraphs, but in entire chapters, convoluted and strung together by breathless "ands," "buts" and "anyways." We seldom asked questions for fear of opening the faucet. Instead, we listened, playing polite audience, nodding at appropriate moments even as we calculated how to steer her back to the subject (if we could remember it) or blurt out a quick thought of our own. "Oh, I *know* I talk too much," she would sometimes sigh. "Your mother tells me I do."

While Grandma could not listen and Page could not talk, they understood each other perfectly. In his silent fortress, Page was unaware of the impenetrable wall of words Grandma built around herself. She kissed him and smiled at him and, more important, accepted him just as he was. She never showed disappointment that he was not "normal," but rather regarded him with fascination, patience and warmth.

One day Page broke a flashlight and brought it to her, hoping she could fix it. I remember her perplexed, earnest face as she fumbled with the cheap plastic gadget. She poked and wiggled the thing and finally, looking sorrowful, shook her head and handed it back to Page. He walked away, to return a few minutes later and try again. She fumbled some more, then gave it back; it was still broken. The next morning Grandma drove to the store and bought him a new one.

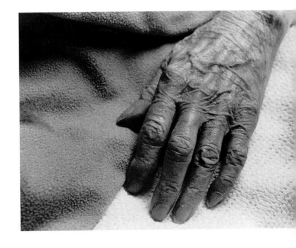

We arrived at the nursing home and stepped into her room. The strokes had left Grandma trembling and unresponsive. The hollow, gaping mask that stared up from her pillow was the face of a wizened stranger. Her mouth hung open. Her wide misty eyes blinked and stared but appeared not to see.

I patted her small, frail hand, and my mind filled with images from a not-so-distant past. This very hand used to produce steaming loaves of the best bread on God's earth. This patient, loving hand didn't stop waving from Grandma's front porch until our car, packed with grandchildren, disappeared around the corner. Now lying limply by her side, her delicate, cool hand felt so soft I was afraid I might accidentally hurt her.

We stood around the bed, smiling uncomfortably, mumbling everything would be all right. My older cousin was the most at ease. "They treatin' you all right in this place, ol' girl?" he asked. I watched her face closely for a sign of recognition. Nothing. Silence didn't suit Grandma.

Stripped of her verbal armor, Grandma seemed exposed, vulnerable and — as I realized with sadness — suddenly approachable. For the first time, I was free to talk all I wanted. But I could think of nothing to say.

"We love you, Grandma," I said finally, wondering if I was reaching her. My words hung in the air, sounding distant and insincere.

Page was standing quietly next to the window, his face brilliant red, tears streaming from his eyes. Just then, he pushed through the group and made his way to the bed. He leaned over Grandma's withered figure and took her cheeks gently in his hands. Head bowed, he stood there for an eternity, cradling her face and soaking her gown with his tears. Those of us with healthy ears were deaf to the volumes being spoken in that wonderful, wordless exchange.

I felt a rush of warmth deep inside me. It surged upward like an inexorable flood, filling my eyes until the room melted in a wash of colors and liquid shapes. As the picture blurred, my perception snapped into brilliant focus. How wrong I had been about Page. Far better than the rest of us, he knew the true meaning of our visit. He knew it perfectly because he grasped it not with his head but with his heart. Like a child unrestrained by propriety or ego, he had the freedom, courage and honesty to reach out in pain to Grandma. This was love, simple and pure.

I saw that Page's condition, for all the grief it brings, is in one sense a remarkable and precious gift. For among the many things my brother was born without is the capacity for insincerity. He cannot show what he does not feel, nor can he suppress urgent emotion. Inside him is a clear channel straight to the center of his soul. As I stood next to him, consumed by his expression of unselfish love, I stopped wondering why Page could not be more like me. At that moment, I wanted to be more like him.

The silence often of pure innocence persuades when speaking fails.

SHAKESPEARE

We kissed Grandma, one by one, and slowly filed out of the room. I was the last to leave. "Bye, Grandma," I said. As I turned to look at her one last time, I noticed her lips come together, as if she was trying to speak. Somehow, if for an instant, she mustered the strength to say good-by. That's when I knew Page had reached her.

That afternoon by Grandma's deathbed, when none of us knew what to say, my speechless brother had said it all.

"I SEE THE MAILBOX"

BY

SUSAN E. BISCHOFF

*T*he chain saw howled as I finished cutting through the branch. I pulled the saw away, and my husband tugged against the other end of the rope that I had tied just above the cut. I almost dropped the saw as I shielded my face from the twigs that brushed by. The branch crashed to the ground, taking my eyeglasses with it. Howard retrieved my glasses and handed them up to me. "Are you okay?" he asked.

"I'm fine," I replied. "Just hot and tired."

"Why don't you take a break?" he urged.

"Come on," I said. "We have only three more trees to trim."

Why had we let this job go for so long? The row of trees we were trimming was supposed to be an eight-foot hedge. Now 20-foot trees, they were threatening the wires.

"I think you should take that smaller branch on the left before the big one in the middle," Howard suggested.

"No," I replied. "I'm going to come down below the fork and get them both with one cut."

"Sue," he said, "I don't think I can keep them both away from the pool screen—they're pretty heavy."

"I'm a lot better than when I started," I said. "I'll make them fall over there." I pointed to a narrow strip of ground between the row of citrus trees and the hedge.

That's when Howard said it: "Honey, I see the mailbox."

"But—" I started to argue. Then, exhaling loudly, I put the chain saw on the ladder's shelf and climbed down.

"I see the mailbox." As we walked into the house, I thought about how many conflicts those words had prevented. To us, they're a code phrase that condenses about 20 minutes' worth of argument into a single line. The story behind the expression is a family saga that gets told over and over.

It had been a beautiful day on Terra Ceia Bay near Bradenton, Fla. We had launched our boat just after sunrise, and the fishing had been excellent. On the road home our sunburns started to hurt, we ran out of cold sodas, and our two daughters started arguing. Soon everyone was cranky and tired.

When we pulled up to the house, the boat had to be carefully backed between the palm tree and mailbox and straight through the small side gate into the back yard. This was never an easy task, but today it seemed even tougher.

Howard made his first attempt, which was too close to the palm tree on his side of the van. He pulled forward and started backing up again. The mailbox, on my side of the van, now seemed too close. "You're too near the mailbox," I said.

He slammed on the brakes, pulled forward and made an adjustment. As the van again backed up, I looked in the mirror and gasped as the boat jackknifed sharply to one side. Howard pulled forward and backed

up once more. This time the boat went straight. I must have gasped again as I turned to check the mailbox, which loomed unexpectedly near. "I SEE THE MAILBOX!" Howard shouted before I could say anything.

I glanced sideways at him. He wasn't even looking at the mailbox; he was looking at the boat. His jaw was clenched tightly, and the grinding motion of his teeth was causing little bulges to move across his temple.

I stuck my head out my window. It surely looked as if the right front bumper was going to snag the metal mailbox post. "I see the mailbox," he repeated, this time in a controlled, even tone.

I considered the situation. The mailbox post and the bumper were only inches apart. No doubt the mailbox was doomed unless I said something. But Howard insisted he saw it, so if I said anything, he'd probably be annoyed at me for hours. Was the mailbox worth it?

No. After all, it hadn't been expensive—it even had some rust around the door hinges. We could replace it with a nicer mailbox—and Howard wouldn't be mad at me.

"I see the mailbox," Howard repeated, just as the bumper grabbed the post. Yanked in by the bumper, the mailbox slammed into the front fender with a loud *thunk*. Howard hit the brakes.

I opened my door and fled into the house. Locking myself in the bathroom, I buried my face in a towel to muffle my uncontrollable laughter. The hysterical sound filled the room despite the towel. I forced myself to think of the gravity of the situation: if Howard wasn't already mad, he surely would be if he heard me laughing, and the mailbox would have been sacrificed in vain. But it was no use—I couldn't stop.

Finally able to compose myself, I went to face Howard. He was sitting in a lawn chair staring at the mailbox, which was still hooked around the bumper. His expression was a vacant, shell-shocked stare.

Before long he stood up and walked over to the boat. He unhooked the trailer from the van and, with surprisingly little effort, pushed the trailer with the boat through the gate into the back yard. What brilliance! Why hadn't we thought of this before?

"I see the mailbox." It means your perspective is gone, you're missing the point, and you're taking risks you shouldn't. Sometimes it even means you're being a jerk. But it's a two-part message, and the second half is always the same: I think I see something you're missing. I would like to stop you before any damage is done, but I love you and don't want to argue or make you mad.

"I see the mailbox" is a truly handy phrase. No marriage should be without it.

MY FOURTEENTH SUMMER

BY

W. W. MEADE

One evening I sat in Miami's Pro Player Stadium watching a baseball game between the Florida Marlins and the New York Mets. During the seventh-inning stretch, I noticed a teenage boy and his father one row in front of me. The father was a Mets fan, by the looks of his cap; his son's bore the Marlins' logo.

The father began ribbing his son about the Marlins, who were losing. The son's responses grew increasingly sharp. Finally, with the Marlins hopelessly behind, the boy turned to his father in a full-bore adolescent snarl. "I hate you!" he said. "You know that!" He spat the words as though they tasted as bad in his mouth as they sounded. Then he got up and took the steps two at a time toward the grandstand.

His father shook his head.

In a moment he stood and squeezed out of his row of seats, looking both angry and bereft. Our eyes met. "Kids!" he said, as though that explained everything.

I sympathized—after all, I was a father now. But I knew how father *and* son felt. There was a time when I, too, had turned on the man who loved me most.

My father was a country doctor who raised Hereford cattle on our farm in southern Indiana. A white four-board fence around the property had to be scraped and painted every three years. That was to be my job the summer after my freshman year in high school. If that wasn't bad enough news, one June day my dad decided I should extend the fence.

We were sitting at the edge of the south pasture, my father thoughtfully whittling a piece of wood, as he often did. He took off his Stetson and wiped his forehead. Then he pointed to a stand of hemlocks 300 yards away. "From here to there—that's where we want our fence," he said. "Figure about 110 holes, three feet deep. Keep the digger's blades sharp and you can probably dig eight or ten a day."

In a tight voice I said I didn't see how I could finish that with all the other stuff I had to do. Besides, I'd planned a little softball and fishing. "Why don't we borrow a power auger?" I suggested.

"Power augers don't learn anything from work. And we want our fence to teach us a thing or two," he replied, slapping me on the back.

I flinched to show my resentment. What made me especially mad was the way he said "our" fence. The project was his, I told him. I was just the labor. Dad shook his head with an exasperated expression, then went back to his piece of wood.

I admired a lot about my dad, and I tried to remember those things when I felt mad at him. Once, when I'd been along on one of his house calls, I watched him tell a sick farm woman she was going to be all right before he left or he wasn't leaving. He held her hand and told her stories. He got her to laugh and then he got her out of bed. She said, "Why, Doc, I do feel better."

I asked him later how he knew she would get better. "I didn't," he said. "But if you don't push too hard and you keep their morale up, most patients will get things fixed up themselves." I wanted to ask why he didn't treat his own family that way, but I thought better of it.

If I wanted to be by myself, I would retreat to a river birch by the stream that fed our pond. It forked at ground level, and I'd wedge my back up against one trunk and my feet against the other. Then I would look at the sky or read or pretend.

That summer I hadn't had much time for my tree. One evening as my father and I walked past it, he said, "I remember you scrunchin' into that tree when you were a little kid."

"I don't," I said sullenly.

He looked at me sharply. "What's got into you?" he said.

Amazingly, I heard myself say, "What the hell do you care?" Then I ran off to the barn. Sitting in the tack room, I tried not to cry.

My father opened the door and sat opposite me. Finally I met his gaze.

"It's not a good idea to doctor your own family," he said. "But I guess I need to do that for you right now." He leaned forward. "Let's see. You feel strange in your own body, like it doesn't work the same way it always had. You think no one else is like you. And you think I'm too hard on you and don't appreciate what you do around here. You even wonder how you got into a family as dull as ours."

I was astonished that he knew my most treacherous night thoughts.

"The thing is, your body is changing," he continued. "And that changes your entire self. You've got a lot more male hormones in your blood. And, Son, there's not a man in this world who could handle what that does to you when you're fourteen."

I didn't know what to say. I knew I didn't like whatever was happening to me. For months I'd felt out of touch with everything. I was irritable and restless and sad for no reason. And because I couldn't talk about it, I began to feel really isolated.

"One of the things that'll help you," my dad said after a while, "is work. Hard work."

As soon as he said that, I suspected it was a ploy to keep me busy doing chores. Anger came suddenly. "Fine," I said in the rudest voice I could manage. Then I stormed out.

When my father said work he meant *work*. I dug post holes every morning, slamming that digger into the ground until I had tough calluses on my hands.

One morning I helped my father patch the barn roof. We worked in silence. In the careful way my father worked, I could see how he felt about himself, the barn, the whole farm. I was sure he didn't know what it was like to be on the outside looking in.

Just then, he looked at me and said, "You *aren't* alone you know."

Startled, I stared at him, squatting above me with the tar bucket in his hand. How could he possibly know what I'd been thinking?

"Think about this," he said. "If you drew a line from your feet down the side of our barn to the earth and followed it any which way, it would touch every living thing in the world. So you're never alone. No one is."

I started to argue, but the notion of being connected to all of life made me feel so good that I let my thoughts quiet down.

As I worked through the summer, I began to notice my shoulders getting bigger. I was able to do more work, and I even started paying some attention to doing it well. I had hated hole-digging, but it seemed to release some knot inside me, as if the anger I felt went driving into the earth. Slowly I started to feel I could get through this rotten time.

One day near the end of the summer, I got rid of a lot of junk from my younger days. Afterward I went to sit in my tree as a kind of last visit to the world of my boyhood. I had to scuttle up eight feet to get space enough for my body. As I stretched out, I could feel the trunk beneath my feet weakening. Something had gotten at it—ants, maybe, or just plain age.

I pushed harder. Finally, the trunk gave way and fell to the ground. Then I cut up my tree for firewood.

The afternoon I finished the fence, I found my father sitting on a granite outcrop in the south pasture. "You thinking about how long this grass is going to hold out without rain?" I asked.

"Yep," he said. "How long you think we got?"

"Another week. Easy."

He turned and looked me deep in the eyes. Of course I wasn't really talking about the pasture as much as I was trying to find out if my opinion mattered to him. After a while he said, "You could be right." He paused and added, "You did a fine job on our fence."

"Thanks," I said, almost overwhelmed by the force of his approval.

"You know," he said, "you're going to turn out to be one hell of a man. But just because you're getting grown up doesn't mean you have to leave behind everything you liked when you were a boy."

I knew he was thinking about my tree. He reached into his jacket pocket and pulled out a piece of wood the size of a deck of cards. "I made this for you," he said.

It was a piece of the heartwood from the river birch. He had carved it so the tree appeared again, tall and strong. Beneath were the words "Our Tree."

An ounce of parent is worth

a pound of the clergy.

SPANISH PROVERB

Leaving the Miami stadium that day, I saw the man and the boy walking toward the parking lot. The man's arm rested comfortably on his son's shoulder. I didn't know how they'd made their peace, but it seemed worth acknowledging. As I passed, I tipped my cap—to them, and to my memories of the past.

Love doesn't just sit there, like a stone, it has to be made, like bread; remade all the time, made new.

URSULA K. LeGUIN

THE DADDY PRIZE

BY

ROBERT FULGHUM

The cardboard box is marked "The Good Stuff." As I write I can see where it is stored on a high shelf in my studio. I like being able to see it when I look up. The box contains those odds and ends of personal treasures that have survived many bouts of "clean-it-out-and-throw-it-away." A thief looking into the box would not take anything — he couldn't get a quarter for any of it. But if the house ever catches on fire, the box goes with me when I run.

One of the keepsakes in the box is a small paper bag. Lunch size. Though the top is sealed with staples and several paper clips, there is a ragged rip in one side through which the contents may be seen.

This particular lunch sack has been in my care for 14 years. But it really belongs to my daughter, Molly. Soon after she came of school age, she became an enthusiastic participant in the morning packing of lunches for herself, her brothers and me. Each bag got a share of sandwiches, apples, milk money and sometimes a note or a treat.

One morning Molly handed me two paper bags. A regular lunch sack. And another with the staples and paper clips. "Why two bags?" I asked.

"The other one is something else."

"What's in it?"

"Just some stuff — take it with you." I crammed both sacks into my briefcase, kissed her and rushed off.

At midday, while hurriedly scarfing down my lunch, I tore open Molly's second bag and shook out the contents. Two hair ribbons, three small stones, a plastic dinosaur, a pencil stub, a tiny seashell, two animal crackers, a marble, a used lipstick, a small doll, two Hershey's Kisses and 13 pennies.

I smiled. How charming. Rising to hustle off to the important business of the afternoon, I swept the desk clean. Into the wastebasket went my leftover lunch and Molly's junk. There wasn't anything there I needed.

That evening Molly stood beside me while I was reading the paper. "Where's my bag?" she asked.

"I left it at the office. Why?"

"I forgot to put this note in it." She handed me a piece of paper. "Besides, I want it back."

"Why?"

"Those are my things in the sack, Daddy, the ones I really like. I thought you might like to play with them, but now I want them again. You didn't lose the bag, did you, Daddy?" Tears puddled in her eyes.

"Oh, no," I lied, "I just forgot to bring it home."

"Bring it tomorrow, okay?"

"Sure thing — don't worry." As she hugged my neck with relief, I unfolded the note she had given me: "I love you Daddy."

I looked long at the face of my child. Molly had given me her treasures. All that a seven-year-old held dear. Love in a paper sack. And not only had I missed it, I had thrown it in the wastebasket. Dear God. I felt my Daddy Permit was about to run out.

It was a long trip back to the office. But there was nothing else to be done. Just ahead of the janitor, I picked up the wastebasket and poured the contents onto my desk. As I was sorting it all out, the jani-

tor came in to do his chores. "Lose something?" I couldn't feel any more of a fool than I was already, so I told him.

"I got kids too," he said. So the brotherhood of fools searched the trash and found the jewels, and we smiled at each other. You are never alone in these things. Never.

After washing the mustard off the dinosaur and spraying everything with breath freshener to kill the smell of onions, I carefully smoothed out the wadded ball of brown paper into a semifunctional bag, put the treasures inside and carried it home gingerly, as if it were an injured kitten.

The next evening I returned it to Molly, no explanations offered. The bag didn't look so good, but the stuff was all there, and that's what counted. After dinner I asked her to tell me about what was in the sack, and so she took out the objects one at a time and placed them in a row on the dining-room table.

It took a long time to tell. Everything had a story. Fairies had brought some of the things. And I had given her the Hershey's Kisses, which she'd kept for when she needed them. I managed to say "I see" very wisely several times in the telling. And, in fact, I did see.

To my surprise, Molly gave the bag to me once again several days later. Same ratty bag. Same stuff inside. I felt forgiven. And trusted. And loved. And a little more comfortable wearing the title of Father. Over several months the bag went with me from time to time, though it was never clear why I did or did not get it on a particular day. I began to think of it as the Daddy Prize and tried to be good the night before so I might be given it the next morning.

In time Molly turned her attention to other things, found other treasures, grew up. Me? I was left holding the bag. She gave it to me one morning and never asked for its return. I have it still.

Sometimes I think of all the times in this sweet life when I must have missed the affection I was being given. A friend calls this "standing knee-deep in the river and dying of thirst."

So the worn paper sack is there in the box. Left over from a time when a child said, "This is the best I've got. Take it — it's yours."

I missed it the first time. But it's my bag now.

CHRISTMAS
LOST AND FOUND

BY

SHIRLEY BARKSDALE

Christmas was a quiet affair when I was growing up. There were just my parents and me. I vowed that someday I'd marry and have six children, and at Christmas my house would vibrate with energy and love.

I found the man who shared my dream, but we had not reckoned on the possibility of infertility. Undaunted, we applied for adoption and, within a year, he arrived.

We called him our Christmas Boy because he came to us during that season of joy, when he was just six days old. Then nature surprised us again. In rapid succession we added two biological children to the family — not as many as we had hoped for, but compared with my quiet childhood, three made an entirely satisfactory crowd.

As our Christmas Boy grew, he made it clear that only he had the expertise to select and decorate the Christmas tree each year. He rushed the season, starting his gift list before we'd even finished the Thanksgiving turkey. He pressed us into singing carols, our froglike voices contrasting with his musical gift of perfect pitch. Each holiday he stirred us up, leading us through a round of merry chaos.

24

Our friends were right about adopted children not being the same. Through his own unique heredity, our Christmas Boy brought color into our lives with his irrepressible good cheer, his bossy wit. He made us look and behave better than we were.

Then, on his 26th Christmas, he left us as unexpectedly as he had come. He was killed in a car accident on an icy Denver street, on his way home to his young wife and infant daughter. But first he had stopped by the family home to decorate our tree, a ritual he had never abandoned.

Grief-stricken, his father and I sold our home, where memories clung to every room. We moved to California, leaving behind our friends and church.

In the 17 years that followed his death, his widow remarried; his daughter graduated from high school. His father and I grew old enough to retire, and in December 1986 we decided to return to Denver.

We slid into the city on the tail of a blizzard, through streets ablaze with lights. Looking away from the glow, I fixed my gaze on the distant Rockies, where our adopted son had loved to go in search of the perfect tree. Now in the foothills there was his grave — a grave I could not bear to visit.

We settled into a small, boxy house, so different from the family home where we had orchestrated our lives. It was quiet, like the house of my childhood. Our other son had married and begun his own Christmas traditions in another state. Our daughter, an artist, seemed fulfilled by her career.

While I stood staring toward the snowcapped mountains one day, I heard a car pull up, then the impatient peal of the doorbell. There stood our granddaughter, and in her gray-green eyes and impudent grin I saw the reflection of our Christmas Boy.

Behind her, lugging a large pine tree, came her mother, stepfather and ten-year-old half brother. They swept past us in a flurry of laugh-

ter; they uncorked wine and toasted our homecoming. They decorated the tree and piled gaily wrapped packages under the boughs.

"You'll recognize the ornaments," said my former daughter-in-law. "They were his. I saved them for you."

When I murmured, in remembered pain, that we hadn't had a tree for 17 years, our cheeky granddaughter said, "Then it's time to shape up!"

They left in a whirl, shoving one another out the door, but not before asking us to join them the next morning for church and for dinner at their home.

"Oh," I began, "we just can't."

"You sure as heck can," ordered our granddaughter, as bossy as her father had been. "I'm singing the solo, and I want to see you there."

We had long ago given up the poignant Christmas services, but now, under pressure, we sat rigid in the front pew, fighting back tears.

Then it was solo time. Our granddaughter's magnificent soprano voice soared, clear and true, in perfect pitch. She sang "O Holy Night," which brought back bittersweet memories. In a rare emotional response, the congregation applauded in delight. How her father would have relished that moment.

We had been alerted that there would be a "whole mess of people" for dinner — but 35! Assorted relatives filled every corner of the house; small children, noisy and exuberant, seemed to bounce off the walls. I could not sort out who belonged to whom, but it didn't matter. They all belonged to one another. They took us in, enfolded us in joyous camaraderie. We sang carols in loud, off-key voices, saved only by that amazing soprano.

Sometime after dinner, before the winter sunset, it occurred to me that a true family is not always one's own flesh and blood. It is a climate of the heart. Had it not been for our adopted son, we would not now be surrounded by caring strangers who would help us hear the music again.

Later, our granddaughter asked us to come along with her. "I'll drive," she said. "There's a place I like to go." She jumped behind the wheel of the car and, with the confidence of a newly licensed driver, zoomed off toward the foothills.

Alongside the headstone rested a small, heart-shaped rock, slightly cracked, painted by our artist daughter. On its weathered surface she had written "To my brother, with love." Across the crest of the grave lay a holly-bright Christmas wreath. Our No. 2 son, we learned, sent one every year.

As we stood by the headstone in the chilly but somehow comforting silence, we were not prepared for our unpredictable granddaughter's next move. Once more that day her voice, so like her father's, lifted in song, and the mountainside echoed the chorus of "Joy to the World," on and on into infinity.

When the last pure note had faded, I felt, for the first time since our son's death, a sense of peace, of the positive continuity of life, of renewed faith and hope. The real meaning of Christmas had been restored to us. Hallelujah!

HELPING FRIENDS
WHO GRIEVE

BY
LOIS DUNCAN

Two years ago our daughter Kaitlyn, 18, was the victim of what police term a "random shooting." My husband, Don, and I were summoned to the emergency room at midnight. Kait was in a coma. She didn't regain consciousness and died the next evening.

I have few clear memories of the 24 hours that Kait clung to life, but I do remember we were not alone. One friend arrived with a sack of quarters so we could make calls from the pay phone. Others met our out-of-town children at the airport and drove them to the hospital. A neighbor took care of the dog.

Until the loss of our daughter, I didn't know how to act when confronted with tragedy. Afraid to do more harm than good, I held myself at arm's length when friends were hurting. I sent cards and flowers, telling myself they knew I was available if they wanted me. Nobody ever called to say I was needed.

I realize now that people in crisis need others around them. It's better to do something klutzy than to do nothing — and the kindest words are often the simplest.

Here's some advice I wish I'd been given when heartbreak was a stranger:

Don't be afraid to intrude. This was my worst fear. Reluctant to barge in where I might not be welcome, I'd withdraw in the mistaken belief that people experiencing tragedy need privacy.

I recall the way I copped out on a teaching colleague. When she was hospitalized with cancer, I made a duty visit. It was stilted and awkward. How do you converse with one so ill? It seemed callous to chat about everyday matters. I waited another week before visiting again. But I had spared only myself. This time I found her room empty — she had died.

Another cancer victim told me, "During the worst of my illness, people who visited regularly were my lifelines. They didn't have to stay long or make conversation. Just knowing they cared enough to stop by my room kept me from feeling alone and forgotten."

Take the initiative. Your friend may be suffering too much to know what he or she needs. The first person to arrive on our doorstep after Kait died was a recent widow still adjusting to her own loss. She took one look at our faces, then loaded us into her car to shop for a cemetery plot. Other friends took over our phone and answered the door. One neighbor mowed our lawn; another put up incoming relatives.

None of these people waited to be asked to help. They saw what needed to be done and did it.

Don't say "I know how you feel." We heard this a lot, and it didn't go down well. "You *can't* know how I feel!" I wanted to scream. "You're not Kait's mother!" Even people who had experienced similar tragedies had not lost *this particular child* in *this particular way.*

I did find it helpful, however, when the mother of a girl who had committed suicide described her own slow, painful return to normal living. "At times I thought I had gone round the bend," she confided. "I'd hear my daughter's footsteps in the hall or her voice singing in the bathroom. One day I even fixed lunch for her. I sat at the kitchen table, eating my sandwich, pretending she was across from me eating hers. It was something I needed to do to keep myself sane."

I found this account reassuring when I went into my own "crazy time," waking night after night to the phantom shriek of the telephone summoning us to the hospital. The dead girl's mother didn't preface her story with "I know how you feel." She simply told me how things were for her and let me relate to them.

Don't look for a silver lining. Efforts to minimize tragedy are not only ineffective, they deposit a truckload of guilt on the person who is suffering.

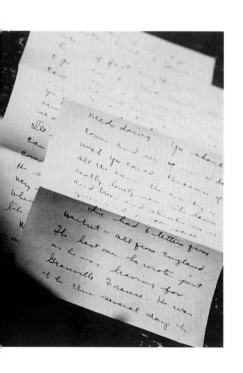

"You have other wonderful children," one woman reminded us. "Imagine how awful it would have been if Kait had been an only child!" Another acquaintance — believe it or not, a psychologist — said, "At least you know your daughter's struggles are over."

Of course I was grateful for the family I still had, but that had no bearing on the fact we'd lost Kait. Was I expected to rejoice that Kait's "struggles" were over, when her life was just starting?

It was also hard to be told "This is God's will." While it's natural to want to share your faith, do so very gently — and only when your friend brings up the subject.

Write a letter of condolence. Store-bought cards don't take the place of a personal letter, no matter how short or awkwardly worded. Every member of our family has drawn strength from the sympathy letters we received.

The most meaningful letters described happy memories. An elderly neighbor remembered our daughter as a six-year-old who "hung a May basket on my doorknob, rang my bell, then hid in the bushes giggling." A junior-high-school classmate recalled Kait's valiant efforts to water-ski. "She'd fall and get up, fall and get up," the girl remembered. "She was tired and freezing, but she wouldn't give up for anything." One note came from a serviceman who'd been Kait's pen pal. He wrote, "Your daughter was bright and funny and had such intriguing views on things. I feel sunlight has gone out of my life."

Those letters told us not only that people cared, but that Kait's life — though short — had affected the lives of others.

Recognize that recovery takes time. For months after Kait's death, I'd lie on my bed by the hour, unable to focus my mind. Just the shopping and housework took all the energy I could muster.

Well-meaning friends asked, "When are you going back to work?" It was hard to convince them that I was too drained to be productive and that, when the time was right, I'd know it.

Be there to listen. Your presence and your willingness to listen are the two most precious gifts you can offer. The people we found most comforting made no attempt to distract us from our grief. Instead, they encouraged Don and me to describe each excruciating detail of our nightmare experience over and over. That repetition diffused the intensity of our agony and made it possible for us to start the healing.

Working through grief is a long, slow process. It may even take years. What helps is the little things — replenishing groceries, cashing checks, returning library books. Most of all, caring enough to help others bear the unbearable.

I'm working again, and Don and I are rebuilding our lives. We're starting to make plans for the future. "Two steps forward," we tell ourselves, "for every step back."

We've come a long way — thanks to the help of our friends.

THE UGLIEST CAT IN THE WORLD

BY

PENNY PORTER

The first time I ever saw Smoky, she was on fire. My three children and I had arrived at the dump outside our Arizona desert town to throw out the weekly trash. As we approached the pit, which was smoldering, we heard the most mournful cries of a cat entombed in the smoking rubble.

Suddenly a large cardboard box, which had been wired shut, burst into flames and exploded. With a long, piercing meow, the animal imprisoned within shot into the air like a flaming rocket and dropped into the ash-filled crater.

"Mommy, do something!" three-year-old Jaymee cried as she and Becky, six, leaned over the smoking hole.

"It can't possibly be alive," Scott, 16, said. But the ashes moved, and a tiny kitten, charred almost beyond recognition, miraculously struggled to the surface and crawled toward us in agony. "I'll get her!" Scott yelled. As he wrapped the kitten in my bandanna, I wondered why it didn't cry from the added pain. Later we learned we had heard its last meow only moments before.

Back at our ranch, we were doctoring the kitten when my husband, Bill, came in, weary from a long day of fence-mending. When he saw our patient, that familiar "Oh, no, not again!" look crossed his face. This wasn't the first time we had greeted him with an injured animal. Though Bill always grumbled, he couldn't bear to see any living creature suffer. So he helped by building perches, pens and splints for the skunks, rabbits and birds we brought home. This was different, however. This was a cat. And Bill, very definitely, did not like cats.

What's more, this was no ordinary cat. Where fur had been, blisters and a sticky black gum remained. Her ears were gone. Her tail was cooked to the bone. Gone were the claws that would have snatched some unsuspecting mouse. Gone were the little paw-pads that would have left telltale tracks on our car. Nothing that resembled a cat was left — except for two huge cobalt-blue eyes begging for help. What could we do?

Suddenly I remembered our aloe vera plant, and its supposed healing power on burns. So we peeled the leaves, swathed the kitten in slimy aloe strips and gauze bandages, and placed her in Jaymee's Easter basket. All we could see was her tiny face, like a butterfly waiting to emerge from a cocoon.

Her tongue was severely burned, and the inside of her mouth was so blistered that she couldn't lap, so we fed her fluids with an eyedropper. After a while, she began eating by herself. We named her Smoky.

Three weeks later, we coated Smoky with a salve that turned her body a curious shade of green. Her tail dropped off. Not a hair remained. And the children and I adored her.

Bill didn't. And Smoky despised him. The reason: Bill was a pipe smoker armed with matches and butane lighters. When he lit up, Smoky panicked, knocking over cups and lamps before fleeing into the open air duct in the spare bedroom.

In time, Smoky became more tolerant. She'd lie on the sofa and glare at Bill as he puffed away. One day he looked at me and chuckled, "Damn cat makes me feel guilty."

As Smoky's health improved, we marveled at her patience with the girls, who dressed her in doll clothes and bonnets so the "no ears" wouldn't show. Then they held her up to the mirror so she could see "how pretty" she was.

By the end of her first year, Smoky resembled a well-used welding glove. Scott was famous among his friends for owning the ugliest pet in the county — probably, the world.

Smoky longed to play outside where the sounds of birds, chickens and chipmunks tempted her. When it was time to feed our outdoor pets, including our Mexican wolf, the occasional skunks and assorted lizards, she sat inside, spellbound, with her nose pressed against the window. It was the barn cats, however, that caused her tiny body to tremble with eagerness. But since she had no claws for protection, we couldn't let her go outside unwatched.

Occasionally we took Smoky on the porch when other animals weren't around. If she was lucky an unsuspecting beetle or June bug would make the mistake of strolling across the concrete. Smoky would stalk, bat and toss the bug until it flipped onto its back, where, one hopes, it died of fright before she ate it.

Slowly, oddly, Bill became the one she cared for the most. And before long, I noticed a change in him. He rarely smoked in the house now, and one winter night, to my astonishment, I found him sitting in his chair with the leathery little cat curled up on his lap. Before I could comment, he mumbled a curt "She's probably cold — no fur you know." But Smoky, I reminded myself, liked being cold. Didn't she sleep in front of air ducts and on the cold brick floor? Perhaps Bill was starting to like this strange-looking animal just a bit.

Not everyone shared our feelings for Smoky, especially those who had never seen her. Rumors reached a group of self-appointed animal protectors, and one day one of them arrived at our door.

"I've had numerous calls and letters," the woman said. "All these dear souls are concerned about a poor little burned-up cat you have in your house. They say," her voice dropped an octave, "she's suffering." Perhaps it should be put out of its misery?

I was furious. Bill was even more so. "Burned she was," he said, "but suffering? Look for yourself."

"Here kitty," I called. No Smoky. "She's probably hiding," I said, but our guest didn't answer. When I turned and looked at her, the woman's skin was gray, her mouth hung open and two fingers pointed.

Magnified tenfold in all her naked splendor, Smoky glowered at the visitor from her hiding place behind our 150-gallon aquarium. The effect was awesome. Instead of the "poor little burned-up suffering creature" the woman had expected to see, a veritable tyrannosaurus Smoky leered at her through the green aquatic maze. Her open jaws exposed saber-like fangs that glinted menacingly in the neon light. Moments later the woman was gone — smiling now, a little embarrassed and greatly relieved.

During Smoky's second year, a miraculous thing happened. She began growing fur. Tiny white hairs, softer and finer than the down on a chick, gradually grew over three inches long, transforming our ugly little cat into a wispy puff of smoke.

Bill continued to enjoy her company, though the two made an incongruous pair — the big weather-worn rancher driving around with an unlit pipe clenched between his teeth, accompanied by the tiny white ball of fluff. When he got out of the truck to check the cattle, he left the air conditioner on for her comfort. Or he picked her up and held her against his denim jacket.

Smoky was three years old on the day she went with Bill to look for a missing calf. Searching for hours, he would leave the truck door open when he got out to look. The pastures were parched and crisp with dried grasses and tumbleweed. A storm loomed on the horizon, and still no calf. Discouraged, without thinking, Bill reached into his pocket for his lighter and spun the wheel. A spark shot to the ground and, in seconds, the weeds were on fire.

Frantic, Bill didn't think about the cat. Only after the fire was under control and the calf found did he return home and remember. "Smoky!" he cried. "She must have jumped out of the truck! Did she come home?"

No. And we knew she'd never find her way home from two miles away. To make matters worse, it had started to rain — so hard we couldn't go out to look for her.

Bill was distraught, blaming himself. We spent the next day searching, knowing she'd be helpless against predators. It was no use.

Two weeks later Smoky still wasn't home. We assumed she was dead by now, for the rainy season had begun, and the hawks, wolves and coyotes had families to feed.

Then came the biggest rainstorm our region had had in 50 years. By morning, flood waters stretched for miles, marooning wildlife and cattle on scattered islands of higher ground. Frightened rabbits, raccoons, squirrels and desert rats waited for the water to subside, while Bill and Scott waded knee-deep, carrying bawling calves back to their mamas and safety.

The girls and I were watching intently when suddenly Jaymee shouted, "Daddy! There's a poor little rabbit over there. Can you get it?"

The love we give away is the only love we keep.

ELBERT HUBBARD

Bill waded to the spot where the animal lay, but when he reached out to help the tiny creature, it seemed to shrink back in fear. "I don't believe it," Bill cried. "It's Smoky!" His voice broke. "Little Smoky!"

My eyes ached with tears when that pathetic little cat crawled into the outstretched hands of the man she had grown to love. He pressed her shivering body to his chest, talked to her softly, and gently wiped the mud from her face. All the while her blue eyes fastened on his with unspoken understanding. He was forgiven.

Smoky came home again. The patience she showed as we shampooed her astounded us. We fed her scrambled eggs and ice cream, and to our joy she seemed to get well.

But Smoky had never really been strong. One morning when she was barely four years old, we found her limp in Bill's chair. Her heart had simply stopped.

As I wrapped her body in one of Bill's red neckerchiefs and placed her in a child's shoe box, I thought of the many things Smoky had taught us about trust, affection and struggling against the odds when everything says you can't win. She reminded us that it's not what's outside that counts — it's what's inside, deep in our hearts.

That's why Smoky will always be in my heart. And why, to me, she'll always be the most beautiful cat in the world.

The supreme happiness of life is the conviction that one is loved; loved for oneself, or better yet, loved despite oneself.

VICTOR HUGO

DOC TENNEY'S
HEALING MAGIC

BY
ALLEN M. SCHOEN AND PAM PROCTOR

For as long as I can remember, I wanted to be a veterinarian. I wanted to work in the country-side, far from the Queens, N.Y., neighborhood where I was raised.

Following my graduation from veterinary school at Cornell University, I signed up as the fourth vet in a practice headed by Forrest Tenney in rural Peterborough, N.H. At the time, Doc Tenney was nearing 70 and had achieved almost legendary stature as an animal healer in New England. To cure his patients, he relied on a palette of remedies that included modern science, folk medicine and plain common sense.

Once, the story goes, Doc Tenney showed up at a barn to treat a cow and was told that the animal had just died. Administering his own version of CPR, he threw himself on top of the prostrate cow and jolted her into taking a breath. Then he gave her a shot of epinephrine, a heart stimulant, and the cow started to come around.

By the time I got to know him, Doc Tenney wasn't up to such physical feats, and as the youngest member of the practice, I became the one

40

who backed him up. "Shawn," he would say, giving an Irish twist to my last name, "I've got a cow calving in a field. Why don't you come along?"

I soon realized on these rounds that Doc Tenney was more than just an experienced veterinarian at work. He was a remarkable healer, whose very presence charmed and soothed human and animal alike. His physical size wasn't particularly striking. Even though he was solidly built, he was only about five-foot-eight. The compelling thing about him was his tender touch.

He would arrive at a barn, give the owner a comforting pat on the shoulder and immediately put him at ease. "There, there," he'd say soothingly. "Everything's going to be all right. I'm just going to give your horse a shot or two and she'll be fine." Then he would walk over to the forlorn animal, and without giving a thought to whether it might kick or bite, he'd gently administer a shot.

The results were extraordinary—it was as though he had passed a magic wand over the creatures under his care. We used to joke that Doc Tenney didn't even need to give an injection. All he had to do was shake a bottle at an animal and it seemed to recover.

Doc Tenney had a storehouse of treatments I had never heard of in vet school. Tucked away in his office were dozens of dusty amber bottles filled with herbal remedies. I learned that if my black bag of sophisticated treatments failed to work, I could always count on Doc Tenney to dig into the arcane insights of the past for a solution.

His willingness to shift strategy from the purely scientific to the utterly unorthodox stood me in good stead when a colleague dispatched me to tend to a sick cow owned by a former biker. "I must warn you," my colleague said ominously, "that the last three vets were thrown off the property."

With my heart beating wildly, I hopped in my car and headed north. I could almost picture my impending fate headlined in the local paper: "Vet Decked by Irate Biker." I was as tense as a banjo string by the time I reached the farm.

It wasn't a big spread, just an old back yard with a dozen or so cows. As I pulled into the driveway, I spotted a man about six-foot-four with a long gray ponytail, sleeveless black T-shirt and tattoos all over his arms. We stopped a few feet from each other, and the biker looked me in the eye. "The doc sent *you*, huh?"

I mustered a weak grin. "Yes, what's the problem?"

"That cow over there," he said. "She's off her feed."

I headed over to the sick cow. She looked awful, her eyes filled with pain. I pulled out my stethoscope. Her heart was beating faster than normal, and her breathing was unusually rapid and shallow. When she exhaled, I could hear a faint grunting sound. Her manure was loose and watery; her breath was sweet—a sign of abnormal blood-sugar levels.

The symptoms suggested she had eaten a foreign object along with her hay, causing her digestion to go awry. It might have lodged in her second stomach, the reticulum, possibly piercing the wall and endangering her heart.

The biker loomed over my shoulder. I couldn't bring myself to spit out the scientific diagnosis, "traumatic reticuloperitonitis," in front of a guy with tattoos on his arms. That might lead to real trouble. From Doc Tenney I had learned to treat the owner as well as the patient. I said, "The cow's got hardware disease. She must have swallowed a nail or something, and it's stopping her from eating."

Instead of being angry, the biker immediately broke into a big grin. "That's what I like to hear," he said, pounding me on the back. "The other vets who came here gave me some highfalutin name for a disease—

42

and the cow *still* died. If my cow's got a nail in her stomach, I want to know it. Go ahead and try to fix it."

I wasn't so sure he'd like the next step. I had to shoot a magnet into the cow's stomach with a balling gun, a device for administering pills. The magnet would stay in her stomach permanently, attracting the nail and any other metal objects that had been swallowed inadvertently. But before I could do this, I had to check for the presence of a magnetic field. I took out a compass and held it under her abdomen.

"Hey, Doc," the biker said, "whatcha doing?" I took a deep breath and, as calmly as I could, explained that if the cow already had a magnet inside her, a second magnet could cause more harm than good. The two magnets could catch a piece of her stomach between them and might cause irreparable damage to the organ.

By now he was getting so fascinated that he eagerly crouched next to me to watch. The compass didn't budge—no other magnet was inside. So I put the balling gun in the cow's mouth and shot a magnet into her stomach. Before leaving, I administered intravenous fluids and medications. "Call me tomorrow," I said. "I'm sure she's going to be fine."

As I got behind the wheel, I could feel my shoulders drop in relief. I hadn't been thrown off the farm, and it seemed that the biker and I might even become friends.

The next day he called with good news. "The cow's eating again!" he said. By following Doc Tenney's lead, I had clearly passed my first real challenge as a vet, but it was the biker who presented me with another when he called weeks later.

"Do you think you could check one of my other cows?" he asked. "My Jersey isn't putting any weight on her leg—and I'm worried."

The lame cow's name was Tammy, and her enormous soft brown eyes looked anxious. I understood why the minute I started gently to palpate her joints and lower back.

"I think she's got a displaced hip," I said. The ligaments holding her hip joint in place had been torn, causing the ball of the femur to slip out of the socket. The result was that whenever she tried to walk on her right rear leg, she cringed in pain.

"This cow was born six years ago on the same day as my daughter," he told me. "The girl loves this cow. I just can't send her away. You've got to help."

I scanned my memory for something—anything—that might work. But my years of scientific training and all that textbook knowledge came up short. My only hope was Doc Tenney. When I called him, he just happened to know of a time-tested remedy. "Take some diluted iodine and inject it into three points on the hip," he said, describing how the three points form a triangle around the hip joint. "I don't know why it works. It just does."

Years later, I discovered that the three points Doc Tenney had described are actually important acupuncture points. The iodine acts as an irritant, increasing circulation in the affected area. Scar tissue then builds up around the points where the needle was inserted, enabling the cow to walk.

Not knowing this at the time, I simply followed Doc Tenney's instructions. Then, as my mentor would have done, I gave the concerned farmer and father a comforting pat on the shoulder. "She's going to be all right," I assured him, trying my best to project an air of confidence.

Sure enough, within a few days the cow was able to put her leg down without wincing. After a week, she was walking around the fields.

This latest experience set off questions within me about the practice of my profession. I had always been a little rebellious, looking for answers when others said there were none. But the success of the iodine injections gave me more tangible evidence that Doc Tenney's approach was right: miracles were available that no textbook had ever recorded. From then on, I was on a perpetual adventure of discovery.

Ironically, the case that may have done the most to establish my reputation in Peterborough seemed fairly straightforward. A pregnant cow was having a difficult time delivering, and the farmer had called for help. When I arrived at the barn, I lathered up my right arm with disinfectant and pulled on my shoulder-length rubber gloves to do an internal exam. As I felt for the calf, it was apparent that the uterus was severely twisted—about 90 degrees from its normal position—cutting off the opening to the birth canal. "I'll have to do a C-section," I told the farmer.

"Naw," he said, "I don't want to pay for that. This isn't one of my best cows. I'll just ship her."

I winced at his bluntness. Dairy farming is a business, and some cows are simply worth more dead than alive. Still, I wasn't there just for the farmer. I had become a vet because I loved animals; if I wanted to keep this cow and her calf alive, I had to think fast.

"You know," I said offhandedly, "there's an old technique that might save the cow and not cost you much." The farmer nodded his head in approval.

"Do you have a wide plank?" I asked. "Instead of untwisting the uterus, we'll untwist the cow!" What I failed to tell the farmer was that I had never executed the procedure myself—I'd only observed. "I don't know about this," said the farmer suspiciously. But I convinced him he had nothing to lose.

With the help of a few neighbors, we lassoed the cow and pulled her to the ground. She lay on her right side, with her legs pointing out in front of her. I made a ramp of the plank, placing it parallel to her outstretched legs and perpendicular to her body. One end of the plank was on the cow's abdomen over the uterus, the other end on the ground. Then I asked the farmer to stand on the plank atop the cow's uterus. While his weight kept the uterus stationary, his friends and I tugged on

For without risk there is no faith, and the greater the risk, the greater the faith.

SOREN KIERKEGAARD

45

the cow's legs and pulled them up and over, in a 180-degree arc, until she was lying on her opposite side with her legs stretched in the other direction.

The procedure worked. At the opening of the uterus, I could feel the calf's nose and two little feet.

The cow, sensing that she was about to give birth, quickly lumbered to her feet and let out a melodious *moo*. Within seconds, the calf popped out and landed on the ground with a thump. I dipped my scalpel in iodine, then cut and tied the umbilical cord to set the newborn calf free.

The mother lovingly began using her rough tongue to massage the tiny muscles and lick the remains of the amniotic sack from the calf's body. I had witnessed this most natural of maternal acts hundreds of times, but now it took on new meaning. A simple wood plank had saved the life of a mother and her calf.

Such risks defy logic, look foolish and confound the most learned practitioners. And yet, I discovered from Doc Tenney, the risks are part of the fine art of successful veterinary medicine. I learned, too, that sometimes the most powerful balm is that most ancient of remedies: the power of a healing touch.

Spring is when you feel like whistling even

with a shoe full of slush.

DOUG LARSON

THE ANGEL FOR LOST CHILDREN

BY

BARBARA SANDE DIMMITT

Richard Paul Evans was physically and emotionally spent. It was November 1992, and the Salt Lake City advertising executive had come off a breakneck few months of 18-hour days. His home life had suffered. The devoted husband and father ached for time lost with his daughters, six-year-old Jenna and four-year-old Allyson. With Christmas near, he wanted to convey how precious his girls were to him. They loved it when he read to them, so a book written by him from the heart seemed the perfect gift.

Evans began to sketch out the story of a father who pours all his energies into his job, selfishly sacrificing his family along the way. But troubling scenes of a mother mourning the death of a child kept intruding on Evans's thoughts. What did this have to do with his story? he wondered. One night the answer came from a childhood memory.

When Rick Evans was four, he'd found his mother, June, quietly weeping one afternoon in her bedroom. He asked her why. "This would have been Sue's birthday," she said softly. Two years before, the boy knew, his mother had delivered a stillborn daughter. With a child's bewildered empathy, Rick reached out and gave her a hug.

The topic of Sue rarely came up in family conversation after that. Rick's father, with a large family to support, stoically threw himself into running his construction business. If the loss of his daughter weighed on his mind, he never gave the merest hint. But there were times when Rick could tell his mother still mourned.

Now, more than 25 years later, the sister he'd never known seemed mystically real. And he understood how this puzzle piece would fit into his book. The story would deal with the twin tragedies of parenthood: the abrupt loss of a child through death and the slower loss of a child through neglect.

The subject seemed dark, depressing. But Evans, inspired, worked to shape a message of love to his girls and one of healing to his mother.

As the book neared completion, he struggled for an image stark enough to portray a parent's despair at losing a child. He recalled an elderly neighbor's reminiscence about playing in the city cemetery as a child, and seeing a woman come each day to weep beneath a statue of an angel marking a child's grave.

The poignant devotion of the mother and the tender symbolism of the angel struck Evans. After changing some of the elements, he added similar imagery to his book.

The slim volume exceeded Evans's hopes at the family's traditional Christmas Eve celebration. He opened a copy and showed it to his mother, pointing to the dedication: "To Sue." "Mom, I think she gave me the story for you," he said. June Evans took her son into her arms and thanked him in an emotion-choked whisper, as Evans's father, David, stood quietly nearby.

Later, with Jenna and Allyson sitting spellbound, Evans read them the story. Then, pleased at its reception, he put the book on a shelf where it would be handy the next time his daughters wanted to hear it.

The Christmas Box, though, seemed bent on pursuing a different destiny. Bound photocopies Evans gave family members were passed along from friend to friend. Strangers called to tell him how much the book meant to them. Soon local bookstores were calling Evans and asking him for copies.

Urged by readers, Evans sent *The Christmas Box* to local publishers, who quickly rejected it. Evans and his wife, Keri, then risked their own savings to self-publish 8000 copies in August 1993. They had no idea the book's word-of-mouth reputation would rocket it to best-seller lists and draw offers from major New York publishers.

By November local book sales were accelerating, and Evans was regularly attending book signings. At one event, a sad-eyed woman approached him. "Would you like me to autograph a book?" he asked.

She shook her head. "I've read it, but you're not old enough to be the man in the book," she said. "The story isn't true."

"No," he replied. "It's fiction."

"I wanted to lay a flower at the angel," she murmured. Then she drifted away.

Evans was dumbstruck. He recognized the suffering in her face; at virtually every book signing he'd seen the same look on people who talked to him about children they'd lost. They always mentioned how healing *The Christmas Box* was for them. Most found the scene involving the stone angel especially cathartic and comforting. Never had Evans imagined that the absence of a real statue might cause pain.

Troubled, Evans then described his encounter to the book's distributor. "We get lots of calls wanting to know where the angel is," one of the distributor's salesmen said to him.

Now Evans himself wanted to know. He asked his elderly neighbor to show him, but they found only low-lying headstones in the part of the cemetery she remembered. Any statue that might have been there 70 years before was long gone.

To Evans, the angel had been a compelling literary device. Perhaps too compelling. As the book's following grew, people from across the country traveled to Salt Lake City, searching for comfort they'd never find. Evans came to think there was only one thing for him to do: erect a new stone angel for those mourners to visit, and find healing.

Upon hearing his plan, June Evans was deeply moved. "I've never had a place to go to mourn. Sue was never buried; that's the way things were done. I think other people thought it would be easier for your father and me if we just tried to forget."

Evans couldn't fathom how he'd deal with such a loss himself. But he understood that, 30 years before, David Evans would have been more a spectator than a participant in the birthing process. And he'd had to be strong in the face of his daughter's death.

In debt to his parents, David, the father of seven, had been working on a degree in social work, hoping it would lead to steadier income than he'd found in construction. He probably was so concerned about his wife's health and the needs of the family that he willed away any grief about the child.

Yet June was still hurting. Clearly, silence and isolation could preserve, even heighten, the feeling of loss.

Certain that his mother and countless others needed this healing place, Evans focused on finding a suitable angel. In September 1994 he met with Ortho Fairbanks, a well-known sculptor, and his wife, Myrna.

It turned out the Fairbanks family had a special reason to want to get involved; they, too, had lost a child.

The author described his vision of a statue of a child with angel's wings and the dedication he planned to hold in early December. Fairbanks told Evans that a stone statue could take years. A bronze statue with a stonelike patina was the best bet, but even that would usually take six months to a year. However, deeply moved by Evans's mission, Fairbanks promised he'd somehow finish the angel on schedule.

The sculptor kept his word. He enlisted the aid of his son, also a sculptor, and the two worked around the clock. Meanwhile Evans and the cemetery sexton identified land where the statue might be erected. Two days before the deadline, the Christmas Box Angel was ready to be lowered into place overlooking Salt Lake City.

On the evening of December 6, 1994, more than 400 people trudged through rain-slicked snow to the upper slope of the cemetery. Tiny candles, protected by umbrellas and cupped by palms, flickered in the darkness. Local dignitaries spoke, but few in the audience took their eyes from the angel.

She stood slightly larger than life- size atop a granite base. Two spotlights illuminated her outstretched arms from below, casting a glow on her upturned face. Those who looked closely could see the word *Hope* blended into the feathered texture of her right wing.

"Bright angels around my darling shall stand," sang a choir of children, their sweet, unschooled voices carrying over the hillside. "They will guard thee from harms, thou shalt wake in my arms."

Then came the moment Evans had anticipated for months. His petite mother, holding a rose whiter than her own hair, approached the angel. She knelt and gently laid the flower at the angel's base. Looking on, Evans found himself blinking away tears. He watched as she stood

He heals the brokenhearted, and binds up their wounds.

PSALMS 147

52

and turned, her eyes shining in a face smoothed by relief. Evans took his mother in his arms. "Finally," she said, "we have a place for Sue."

People now filed past the angel until white flowers cascaded over the base of the statue like a long-trained skirt. Someone placed a rose across the angel's outstretched palms, and soon the statue's arms were filled. Parents left tiny toys, pictures and other mementos of their children.

Evans stood in the drizzle and watched the angel at work. He had asked Ortho Fairbanks to sculpt an angel with arms raised as if asking to be lifted. But judging by the peaceful expressions on the candlelit faces around him, this angel was reaching out more to comfort than to be comforted. "Come and lay your burdens here," she seemed to be saying. And one by one, her visitors did.

Evans surveyed the crowd, and his eyes once more went to his mother. He'd completed his gift to her and felt as if nothing could surpass this moment. But then he glanced beside her and noticed his father.

Tears were streaming down David Evans's cheeks. In the look of astonished anguish on the older man's face, the son read a tale of suffering long held at bay. Surrounded by strangers drawn close by their common tragedy, Evans's parents turned to each other and embraced. Above them hovered the angel, glistening in the night rain.

HELP YOURSELF THROUGH THE HARD TIMES

BY

COLLIN PERRY

*S*ome years ago I had what most would call the American Dream: a thriving construction business, a comfortable home, two new cars and a sailboat. Moreover, I was happily married. I had it all.

Then the stock market crashed, and suddenly no one was looking at the houses I'd built. Months of murderous interest payments gobbled up my savings. I couldn't make ends meet and lay awake nights in a cold sweat. Just when I thought things couldn't get worse, my wife announced that she wanted a divorce.

With no idea what to do next, I resolved literally to "sail off into the sunset," following the coastline from Connecticut to Florida. But somewhere off New Jersey I turned due east, straight out to sea. Hours later, I climbed up on the stern rail and watched the dark Atlantic slip beneath the hull. *How easy it would be to let the water take me,* I thought.

Suddenly the boat plummeted between two swells, knocking me off-balance. I grabbed the rail, my feet dragging in icy brine, and just managed to haul myself back on board. Shaken, I thought, *What's happening to me? I don't want to die.* From that moment, I knew I had to see things through. My old life was gone. Somehow I'd have to build a new one.

Everyone, at some point, will suffer a loss—the loss of loved ones, good health, a job. "It's your 'desert experience'—a time of feeling barren of options, even hope," explains Patrick Del Zoppo, a psychologist and bereavement specialist with the Archdiocese of New York. "The important thing is not to allow yourself to be stranded in the desert."

So, can we actually do things to help ourselves through bad times? As I discovered, you *can* take charge of your own cure. Here's how:

Let yourself grieve. Counselors agree that a period of grieving is critical. "There's no shame in this," says Del Zoppo. "Tears aren't a sign that you're simply feeling sorry for yourself but are an expression of sadness or emotion that must find an outlet."

And it doesn't matter if the grieving takes a while to surface, as long as it finally finds expression. Consider the case of Donna Kelb of Syracuse, N.Y. One spring day her 16-year-old son, Cliff, Jr., and 15-year-old son, Jimmy, were sanding their boat, preparing it for the season. Suddenly Donna heard a scream. Rushing outside, she found her two sons lying on the ground near the boat.

Jimmy had gone into the water and returned dripping wet. When he picked up the sander, he was electrocuted. Cliff, knocked to the ground by the current when he tried to grab the tool, recovered.

Donna was so numbed by this tragedy that she didn't cry for weeks—not even at the funeral. Then back at work one day, she began to feel dizzy. "Finally I went home, locked myself in my room and just wailed," she says. "It was as though this great weight was being lifted from my shoulders."

What Kelb experienced after her tragic loss was what Del Zoppo calls a "first-line defense that shields the consciousness from some

extremely unpleasant reality." Kelb couldn't begin her healing process until nature had allowed her time to sort out her tragedy.

Understand your anger. "Anger is natural," says Del Zoppo, "but it can be released in a wholesome way." Properly understood, it can serve your recovery.

Candace Bracken's future seemed full of promise. The 25-year-old airline service coordinator had a new baby and a new job. Then one day, she began hemorrhaging uncontrollably. Acute leukemia was diagnosed, and Bracken was given two weeks to live. After the initial shock, she felt angry. "I had taken care of myself, lived a straight and narrow life," says Bracken of Miami. "Things like this weren't supposed to happen to people like me."

She reeled at the thought of her imminent death, and withdrew. "I just gave up," she says. Then a doctor told her she needed to arrange for someone to care for her daughter. "How dare you tell me to find someone else to raise my child!" Bracken snapped. At that moment, she realized that she had strong reasons to fight for her life. Her anger, formerly crippling, now sparked her. It helped see her through a harrowing, but ultimately successful, bone-marrow transplant.

Face the challenge. Another obstacle on the road to health after a significant loss can be denial. Instead of facing what has happened to them, says Dr. Michael Aronoff, psychiatrist and a spokesperson for the American Psychiatric Association, many people "try to fill up that empty feeling looking for an escape." The man who rarely touched a drink will begin hitting the bottle. A woman who watched her weight will overeat. Others—like me—try literally to "run away."

After working for bosses all his life, John Jankowski of Staten Island, N.Y., had always longed to have his own options- and stock-trad-

Whatever does not destroy me makes me stronger.

FRIEDRICH WILHELM NIETZSCHE

ing firm. He finally got the start-up money and did well. Then came a downturn in business, and before long Jankowski was in serious financial trouble.

"It was like I'd run into a brick wall and my whole life had been shattered," he says. With financial resources exhausted and the pressure of a family to support, Jankowski's thoughts turned to escape.

One morning, while on a run, he just kept going. After jogging westward for two hours, he staggered back home. "It finally dawned on me that I couldn't run away from my troubles. The only thing that made sense was to face up to my situation," he says. "Admitting failure was the toughest part—but I had to before I could get on with my life."

Get out and do. "After a few weeks, I urge people recovering from loss to get back into a routine," says psychiatrist and Boston University professor Bessel A. van der Kolk. "It's important to force yourself to concentrate on things other than your hurt." Consider these activities:

Join a support group. Once you've made the decision to "get on with life," you'll need someone to talk to—and the most effective kind of conversation can be with someone else who has undergone an ordeal.

Read. When you can focus after the initial shock, reading—especially self-help books—can offer inspiration as well as relaxation.

Keep a journal. Many find comfort in creating an ongoing record of their experiences. At best it can serve as a kind of self-therapy.

Plan events. The idea that there are things to look forward to reinforces that you are forging ahead into a fresh future. Schedule that trip you've been postponing.

Learn new skills. Take a course at a community college, or take up a new hobby or sport. You have a new life ahead; any new skill will complement it.

Reward yourself. During highly stressful times, even the simplest daily chores—getting up, showering, fixing something to eat—can seem daunting. Consider every accomplishment, no matter how small, a victory to be rewarded.

Exercise. Physical activity can be especially therapeutic. Therese Gump of Chicago felt confused and adrift after her 21-year-old son committed suicide. A friend talked her into taking a jazzercize class. "It was just mindless stretching and bouncing to music," Gump says, "but it made me feel better physically, and when you feel better physically you feel better mentally."

"Exercise gets you out of your head and your troubles," Aronoff explains, "and it allows you to experience your body with your two feet on the ground."

Get outside yourself. "Many people who survive traumatic situations eventually find the need to take meaningful action," says Dr. van der Kolk. "They may start organizations, write books, work for awareness. Along the way they discover that a powerful way to help themselves lies in helping others."

You don't have to suddenly become an organizer to reach out to others. Irene Roberts, a 68-year-old medical secretary in New York City, underwent grueling chemotherapy for ovarian and breast cancer. Throughout the experience, love from her family and friends, as well as prayer, helped Roberts maintain her humor and positive outlook.

Doctors and staff were touched by Roberts's optimism, and when she'd ask how they were feeling, they would respond. "I'd just lie there and listen," she says with a twinkle in her eye, "never letting on that they were helping me more than I was helping them. The truth is that thinking of others rather than spending a lot of time thinking about myself played a huge role in my full recovery."

Be patient with yourself. People often ask, "When will this terrible pain stop?" Experts resist being pinned down to time frames.

"Roughly, it's a minimum of six months before you even start to feel better," says Aronoff. "And it can be as long as a year, possibly two. A lot depends on disposition, the support within your environment, and if you get help and work on it."

So, be easy on yourself. Recognize that you'll need time, and that your own pace of recovery may not fit with that of others. Congratulate yourself at each step through grief: I'm still here, I've made it this far!

Sailing is a slow business. I made it to Florida in five weeks. In attempting to "run away," I'd embarked on a trip that gave me a structure, a daily outdoor routine requiring physical exertion, and plenty of time. I was still hurting, but by the time I anchored in Miami, I was ready to try again. At what, I wasn't sure.

"Why not get back to writing— to what you were trained for?" said my dad over the phone. He was right. And here I am now, writing to you. It feels good to be back.

I'm not afraid of storms, for I'm learning how to sail my ship.

LOUISA MAY ALCOTT

A HUSBAND BEYOND COMPARE

BY

MARY HIGGINS CLARK

On our first date, I asked Warren F. Clark what his middle initial stood for. Without batting an eye he answered, "Fascinating." Two hours later in a Greenwich Village pub he was scribbling names on a cocktail napkin. "I'm making a guest list for the wedding," he said. "Now don't get all girlie and cute. You know we'll be great together."

That was April 29, 1949. We were married on December 26 — a day of gale-swept rain. Rather than arrive at the church looking like a drowned rat, I waited for a break in the torrent and was 22 minutes late.

At the altar, Warr's romantic question was, "What kept you?"

We had five children and lived merrily together until his death 15 years later at the age of 45.

When I sat down to write this tribute to Warr, I found it very difficult to decide what I wanted to say about him. I couldn't be maudlin. Warr was too much fun for that. Even now when his name comes up, the immediate reaction of family or friends is a burst of laughter. So I studied some of the glittering remembrances other people have written about loved ones to get some ideas:

He graduated at the top of his class. That wouldn't do at all. Warr was one of the brightest people I've ever known, but his school record was totally undistinguished. He once got a final grade of 17 in a high-school chemistry course. "When those equations started appearing on the blackboard, I looked up the movie schedule," he explained.

A war hero, he came home covered in glory. Warr was in the first peacetime draft just before Pearl Harbor, but he washed out of pilot training because of colorblindness and spent the next 61 months defending the "shores" of Kentucky and Oklahoma.

His rise in the business world was meteoric. Well, as a matter of fact, it wasn't. One of his first jobs was as a salesman for a steamship company. The problem was that even though he was a born salesman, there were no commissions and the pay was minimal. As he explained, "The side benefits are great. We can take a round-the-world cruise, first-class, every couple of years if I stay here. The only trouble is, I won't be able to afford to tip the steward."

Next, he took a job selling hearing aids. Our first sign that something might be amiss was when he came home with a mortar and pestle, a heater, a jar of wax and some string. He hadn't been told he would have to take a wax impression of a potential buyer's ear.

 Obviously he had to practice taking impressions, so I became his subject. Marilyn, our firstborn, was then six weeks old, and I would sit on the couch feeding her while Warr began experimenting. "Try not to move," he'd caution as he stuffed my ear with globs of melting wax. After the wax hardened, he would pull the string, hoping for a perfect impression. It seldom worked.

Not long after that, he went back to the travel business, where he'd always belonged. At the time of his death, he was regional manager of a charter airline.

He was a husband beyond compare. Now we're getting warm, but not by today's standards, when Mom and Dad share the shopping, the housekeeping, the diaper changing. Our daughter Marilyn was born 39 years ago — when the husband delivered his wife to the hospital and was sent home to get a good night's sleep.

It was a long, hard labor. The following morning I was experiencing two-minute labor pains with 30-second intervals. Warr sat silently, searching for comforting words. At last, during a respite, he said brightly, "Well, at least it doesn't hurt between the pains." I pulled myself up on one elbow. "Out!" I ordered.

When Marilyn was six weeks old, he said, "Look, I'll help with these 2 a.m. feedings. All you have to do is heat the bottle, change her and I'll take over." That night I tried to awaken my sleeping beauty. After ten minutes, Warr finally roused. I handed Marilyn to him and gratefully fell asleep. A few minutes later, I was awakened by a wail. Warr was fast asleep — the baby in his arms and the bottle dripping somewhere near her ear.

He was a father beyond compare. While Warr wasn't a mother's helper, he *was* a wonderful father. He taught his children the gifts of faith, laughter and generosity. He taught them how to take life as it comes and how to enjoy it while it lasts. As manager of a Little League team, he wanted his boys to win. But no matter how untalented a youngster was, he played in every game.

Warr's exasperated exchange with Italian-born Fausto Miraglia, who struck out with awesome consistency, became town folklore. Warr said, "Fausto, I'm going to have you deported." Fausto said, "Mr. Clark, what makes you think they'll take me back?"

He was an inspiration to all who knew him. It was eight months after Patty, our fifth child, was born that the chest pains began. For three weeks we blamed it on a strained muscle. I insisted he see a doctor. A few days later, Warr was told he was a likely candidate for a heart attack. Always have nitroglycerin tablets in your pocket. Never run for a bus. Don't carry a heavy suitcase. Don't roughhouse with the children.

That night, when Warr came home from work, the kids jumped all over him, and I held out the cocktail I had waiting. We toasted each other. Whatever time we had left, we'd make it great.

Warr had three heart attacks in the next five years, but his sense of humor never stopped. "Don't be a blooming widow," he would tell me. "Try to look real gaunt." No one was more graceful in loving life — and leaving it.

He will always be with us. Yes. He's been gone 25 years. The children are raised, but it has always seemed as though he walked with them. Three years after his death, when the boys were in high school, they came home delighted with themselves. "Dad would be proud. We took aptitude tests, and in mechanical ability we both came out untrainable." All five — Marilyn, Warren, David, Carol and Patty — have inherited his quick, sunny wit.

Shortly before his execution, Sir Thomas More is said to have comforted a friend with these words: "I trust that we shall, once in heaven, see each other full merrily." When I get there, I know Warren F. (for Fascinating) Clark will be in the midst of the merriment. More than likely, he'll drape an arm around my shoulders and ask the question he asked at the altar: "What kept you?"

WELCOME CHANGE

BY

VIVIAN BUCHAN

How often have you said, "When my life gets back to normal . . . ," not realizing that life can never get back to any place or time?

Change is the most changeless thing in the universe. We need to accept all change — welcome or unwelcome — with the understanding that nothing comes to stay, but only to pass. And because two things can never occupy the same space at the same time, one change makes way for the next, giving us the opportunity to grow.

Linda was devastated when her husband was transferred to a city a thousand miles from her family and friends. Certain she would be miserable, she resisted bitterly. She secretly wished her husband would go without her.

Then a friend convinced her that although the sun was setting on one life, it would rise on another. So she decided to accept the change as gracefully as possible. To make friends, she joined a painting class. There she discovered a talent she never dreamed she had. Before long, her teacher arranged an exhibition. Linda's work was so well received that she began getting commissions for her seascapes. Soon she was a sought-after watercolorist.

"I was so childish," she wrote to her mother. "This change has given me a chance to develop a talent I never would have discovered."

If we learn to welcome change, if we look for the blessings in it, we will be able to accept the problems and worries of the present, knowing that "this too shall pass."

Remember, one door never closes without another opening.

There is a certain relief in change, even though it be from bad to worse;

as I have found in travelling in a stagecoach,

that it is often a comfort to shift one's position and be bruised in a new place.

—Washington Irving

MY $100 TRUST FUND

BY

JAMES EDWARD PEDERSEN

*T*enth grade had drawn to a close, and Max and I were driving home in his parents' Ford Falcon. It was June 1967 in Port Alberni, a lumber-mill town on Canada's Vancouver Island. As we turned a corner, I spotted my father, the city gardener, wearing his plaid flannel shirt and green work trousers.

"Hey," Max called out, "there's your old man!"

"Keep going!" I said, slinking down to avoid being seen. Earlier that day I'd gotten my report card and learned I would have to repeat a grade. Dad would be terribly disappointed.

After immigrating to Canada from Denmark in 1928, my father had embarked on a lifetime of physical labor. Money never came easily to him, and he wanted his sons to do better. My two brothers had taken his message to heart. Mundi, the oldest, had attended Utah State University and was now married and living in Provo. Laurence was also there, attending Brigham Young University.

At home I put my report card on the table where I knew Mom

would find it before Dad got home. I hoped she would soften the blow. Then I rejoined Max, who, having also flunked tenth grade, was in no great hurry to face his parents either.

Later, when I returned home, my mother said tersely, "Your father wants to see you."

I found him lying on his bed, a mystery novel open face-down on his chest. "Well, I guess I didn't make it, Dad!" I blurted. I was shocked at how cavalierly the words spilled out.

Dad sat up, his face suddenly looking older than his 63 years. "You've really let me down," he said. Like droplets on a hot griddle, my false confidence fizzled and evaporated.

Mumbling "I'm sorry," I fled to the back yard. Moments later I heard footsteps, and then my father crouched beside me. "It's okay, Jimmy," he reassured me. "There's nothing you can do about it now. But you have to make up for it next year."

"I'm sorry, Dad," I said.

"Being sorry isn't enough. Your teachers tell me you could get A's. But all you do is waste your time."

I needed things to be right between Dad and me. As I sensed him pardoning me, I nodded in relief.

When school doors opened the next fall, Beverly Bonfield walked into my homeroom and hurled me into uncharted realms.

She had long, silky hair and innocent eyes, and she carried herself with a shy, quiet dignity. I asked her to be my lab partner, and she agreed. In October I tried to work up the courage to ask her to a school dance. I had one problem: no formal clothes.

I approached Dad as he sat in his easy chair watching TV. "I know we can't afford it," I began hesitantly, "but there's someone I'd like to take to the dance, and I don't have a suit."

He looked at me for a moment. Dad had never given me money for anything he considered frivolous, so I knew I was asking a lot. "You'll have exactly what you need!" he announced.

The next evening we walked into Ralph's Men's Wear. "I'd like to outfit my son for a dance," Dad said to the salesman. "Can we see your best?"

The salesman laid out a black sports jacket, light-gray dress slacks and a white button-down shirt. The jacket alone was $45, an unheard-of sum. I looked at Dad, expecting him to shake his head. But he nodded assent.

I left the store outfitted from coat to shoes. Dad had peeled off well over $100, more money than I had ever seen spent for anything, except maybe a car.

The next Saturday I summoned the nerve to ask Beverly to the dance. "I'm sorry," she said sympathetically. "I have to go to Toronto for a wedding that weekend. But thanks!"

I said good-bye, put down the receiver and let out a primal scream.

"The girl has to go out of town with her family," I later explained, dejectedly, to my father. A little deceitfully, I added, "It was unexpected."

Dad frowned and said in a comforting tone, "There'll be other dances." I was flooded with relief.

A few Sundays later I wore my new outfit to church. After dinner I had settled in to watch TV when Max drove up. "I'm going with Max to the Army drill hall to watch roller hockey!" I yelled to my parents.

"Change your clothes," Dad called.

"We're just going to watch!" I argued, and took off.

But in the drill hall someone yelled to us, "There aren't enough play-ers to make teams! Come on!" So I ditched my jacket, rented skates, and set up as goalie.

Five minutes into the game a sudden shot blasted toward me. Landing hard on my knees, I heard a resounding r-r-r-rip! Both my pant knees were torn from seam to seam.

Panic-stricken, I raced home and stomped into the living room, showing the pants to my shocked parents. "Why didn't you listen?" Dad cried out. "Do you have any idea how long I worked to buy those clothes?" Walking into his bedroom, he closed the door. He had never turned his back to me before.

Chastened but resentful, I wandered into my room, fantasizing about the brilliant defense I could have made.

In a few moments Dad came in. "You played hockey tonight, didn't you?" he asked bluntly. I nodded.

"It's becoming difficult to trust you," he said in a voice filled with pain.

"People put pressure on me, Dad!"

"You've got to stand up for yourself. I won't always be here for you—and the world won't be as forgiving as I've been." I wasn't sure what he meant, but once again I felt a great weight lift when words of encouragement followed his lecture.

After striking out with Beverly, I developed a plan to boost my standing with girls. Nothing attracts them, I thought, like a lead guitarist. I vowed I would own the red Fender Stratocaster in the window of Holloway Records.

My weekend job at the lumber mill always sent me home covered in grease and sawdust, but now the drudgery began to take on new meaning. Slowly my savings grew. One Saturday I finally passed the $100 mark. On Monday, I decided, I'd ask the store manager if a $100 deposit would hold the guitar.

Sunday morning my mother awoke sick, and Dad sent me to church alone. "Drive slowly and come straight home," he said.

"Okay," I promised, exhilarated by the prospect of having our new Datsun sedan to myself. It was only the second new car Dad had ever owned, and the first he had ever bought on credit.

At church I found four friends: Billy Hackwell, Brian McTaggart, Darlene Lowery and Chris Johannessen. "Where are your folks?" Billy asked.

"My mom's sick," I answered. "Dad stayed home with her."

They huddled a moment, then climbed into the car. "Let's drive to Sproat Lake," Darlene suggested. I hesitated, remembering Dad's instructions, but I figured I'd be home early and no one would be the wiser.

The back roads were covered with snow and ice. After a few miles I crested a slippery hill and came face to face with a huge truck in my lane, moving around a stalled car. I jammed on the brakes, and we skidded head-on into the truck.

Getting out, I saw the truck wasn't damaged. But the front of Dad's car was demolished. *Dad will kill me!* I thought.

A tow truck hauled my father's pride and joy home. As soon as we reached the house, my friends jumped out and scattered until just Chris and I were left to face the music.

When he saw the crumpled Datsun, Dad flew out the front door. "What have you done?" he shouted. "Go inside!" Now even Chris decided to leave.

In the house he said disgustedly, "It's not the car—we can fix that. I can't trust you anymore." Once again I retreated to my room to wait for his knock.

Not until evening deepened into nightfall did I realize that this time he wouldn't be coming. As I fell asleep, I knew a gulf had formed between us. And I worried that without another chance I would never close it.

On Dad's instructions I went to the insurance adjuster's office.

"You slid a bit into the opposing lane," the adjuster told me, "so you share partial blame for the collision. Your father has to pay the $100 deductible."

His words shocked me, not only because the truck had been entirely in my lane but because the $100 wiped out almost all my savings for the guitar. As I pulled out my five $20 bills, I thought bitterly of the dirty job I'd been doing every Saturday. Now it all seemed pointless.

Somehow I got through tenth grade, and in 1969 squeaked by the 11th. I was in my bedroom one evening when Dad walked in. Since the accident I'd been struggling with feelings of aimlessness and emptiness. I hung out with friends and squandered my paycheck, and in that time he and I had drifted further apart.

"I've been thinking about your future," he began. "College isn't for everyone. I want you to know that there's no shame in working at the mills."

I sat there stunned and confused. Was he giving up on me? Or was he just saying that he loved me no matter what?

That summer Laurence was home from Brigham Young, earning money for the next semester. One night he asked about my plans.

"Work in the mill, I guess," I said.

"What happens if it closes?" he asked.

"I'll find another job."

"And why would someone hire you?" he asked bluntly. I sat silently.

"Look," he said, "why don't you come to Provo and finish school there? If you don't get out now, I'm afraid you never will."

His words scared me even more than my father's had. Life in Port Alberni was all I knew. But when I considered a fresh start somewhere else, a sense of hope emerged.

Mistakes are a fact of life. It is the response to the error that counts.

NIKKI GIOVANNI

Anxiously I asked my father for permission. "I think once I get away from everything here, I'll do better," I pleaded.

Dad looked me in the eye. He must have seen the desperation. "Okay," he finally said, "I'll see what we can do."

Three weeks later I packed my bags. When I went to say good-bye to Dad, I found him in his bedroom pulling something out of his desk.

"I know you don't have much money," he said as he handed me an envelope. "This might help." I ripped open the envelope. Inside were five wrinkled $20 bills.

"Don't thank me," he said. "It's your money—from your car accident." I felt my face redden. "After you came back from the adjuster, I paid him a visit," Dad explained. "I asked him why he faulted you for hitting a truck in your lane. We both knew he'd taken advantage of you. I demanded he clear your record and pay the deductible back—in your own bills.

"But if I had given the money back to you, you wouldn't have learned anything," he continued. "So I put it away until I felt the time was right."

The boy in me wanted to throw my arms around him. But Dad held out his hand to me the way he did to other men. I sensed that he was giving me the opportunity to win back his trust, once and for all. I was determined not to let him down.

In Provo I tried to concentrate on my 12th-grade studies. I spent my $100 sparingly, mostly on books. Loneliness was a constant problem. Feelings of alienation and discouragement often threatened to break my resolve. Only when I thought of facing Dad again did I find the strength to refocus. And as the months went by, my efforts began to bear fruit.

In April I stared at my third-quarter report card, unable to believe I had gotten straight A's.

I called Dad. "I'm proud of you," he said. "I always knew you could do it." My eyes moistened.

Two months later I graduated and went home. From the moment I walked in, I knew the gulf between me and Dad had disappeared.

Just days after my return Dad suffered a heart attack. He spent the next month and a half in the hospital. On one visit in mid-August, I sat awkwardly, not knowing what to say. He finally broke the silence.

"What are you going to do with your life?" he asked. Sensing his need to know his house was in order, I talked about my future. We spoke not of the dreams of a teen-ager seeking the adulation of friends but of the plans of a man heading for college. Dad seemed content.

That night he left us. I was profoundly thankful that I'd won back the trust I'd so thoughtlessly lost.

In the following years, as I attended college and started a business career, I discovered that Dad was right. The world hasn't been as patient or forgiving as he was. But I also discovered that Dad has never left me. He stood by me—his prodigal son—no matter how many times I stumbled. He looks over me still.

GETTING CONNECTED

BY

THOM HUNTER

*M*y wife Lisa and I were struggling to put out the small weekly newspaper we had dedicated ourselves to producing in Guthrie, Okla. I wrote, and Lisa sold ads. Many nights we'd work well past midnight as the rest of the town and our children slept.

On one such night, we crawled into bed only to crawl back out a few hours later. I ate my cereal, drank a large soda, then headed toward Oklahoma City and the printer. Lisa matched our five children to socks and sent the older three off to school with lunch bags in hand. I was so tired I had no business driving. Lisa was so tired she had no business doing anything.

"It's 70 degrees, and the sun is shining. Another beautiful day," the disc jockey said cheerily on the car radio. I ignored him.

What I couldn't ignore was the need created by the large soft drink. I realized I'd never make it to the city, so I pulled into the rest stop on the interstate just a few miles from our house.

In her exhausted state, meanwhile, Lisa was practicing an all-too-familiar art form: calling utility companies, explaining why the payment was late and begging for one more day of hot water and air conditioning. She looked up the number and dialed—she thought—the electric company.

As I stepped from the car at the rest stop, I heard the public pay phone ringing. I was the only person there, but I still looked all around. "Somebody answer the phone," I shouted, just like at home.

It *had* to be the wrongest of wrong numbers, I thought. Then I heard myself say, "Why not?" I walked to the phone and picked up the receiver.

"Hello?" I said.

Silence. Followed by a shriek.

"Thom! What on earth are you doing at the electric company?"

"Lisa? What on earth are you doing calling the pay phone at a rest stop?"

We went through "I can't believe this" all the way to "this is downright spooky." I expected Rod Serling to come walking past to the "Twilight Zone" theme.

We stayed on the phone, and our exclamations changed to conversation. An unhurried, real conversation, without interruption—our first in a long time. We even talked about the electric bill. I told her to get some sleep, and she told me to wear my seat belt and lay off soda.

Still, I didn't want to hang up. We'd shared a wondrous experience. Even though the numbers of the electric company and the pay phone differed by only one digit, that I was there when Lisa called was so far beyond probability we could only suppose God knew we both needed, more than anything else that morning, each other's voices. He connected us.

That call was the beginning of a subtle change in our family. We both wondered how we had become so devoted to our work that we

could leave our children with a stranger to put them to bed. How could I sit across the breakfast table and never say good morning?

Two years later, we were out of the business that had so dominated our lives, and I had a new job—with the telephone company. Now, tell me God doesn't have a sense of humor.

We pardon in the degree that we love.

LA ROCHEFOUCAULD

A MUTT NAMED MEKO

BY
JACK FINCHER

Her birth in 1953 was difficult. Too little emergency oxygen had been pumped into her small body, damaging immature nerves and leaving Ellen Richau partially deaf. Worse, her doctors in Billings, Mont., said the deafness would increase as Ellen grew older.

Watching their golden-haired daughter play with her two brothers, Jan and Lavio Richau came to a decision: they would not send her to a school for the deaf. "Your father and I feel you should grow up in the hearing world," her mother told her. "You're smart, Ellen. You can make it."

Ellen tried. And, gradually, she became so skilled at lip reading that her father, a cabinetmaker, often forgot her handicap. But once she started school, everything changed.

Classmates thought Ellen was retarded, and they ignored or taunted her. And once, when she missed a command to clear her desk, the teacher slapped Ellen's hands with a ruler. Humiliated, she broke down in tears. The shy little girl drew deeper into herself.

While in grammar school, Ellen was fitted with a clunky hearing aid. The primitive electronics amplified not only speech but the drone of passing cars and the whistle of the prairie wind. One day in class, the device began shrieking. Ellen couldn't hear it, but the other students covered their ears, laughing and pointing.

From then on, the moment she left home in the morning, Ellen stuffed the hearing aid in her book bag and retreated into silence. If something challenged or confronted her, she turned her back on it. When one of her watercolors won a prize, bringing her into contact with others, she quit painting.

In her teens, Ellen met John Raines, a young ranch hand. Before long, she dropped out of school, married John and went to work on their small farm. Then an auto accident accelerated her hearing loss. Soon after, the couple was divorced.

Ellen was determined to build a home for her two babies and, for a time, came out of her shell. She passed the high-school equivalency exam, earned an accounting degree and went to work as a bookkeeper. She even took up ballroom dancing, feeling the beat through the floor and mouthing the lyrics to keep time.

Tests at this point showed her hearing was 95-percent gone. Complications from a series of kidney operations, together with her pain medication, caused her to give up her job. After a rapid weight gain, she also gave up dancing and, once more, withdrew into her private world.

Then one day in 1985 Ellen saw a magazine ad in her audiologist's office about dogs trained to help the deaf the way guide dogs help the blind. *Why not?* Ellen wondered. *I love animals. What do I have to lose?*

She got in touch with Dogs for the Deaf, Inc., a national nonprofit organization in Oregon that trains such dogs. There was a long waiting list, but after 15 months Ellen was assigned a dog. Soon an unlikely twosome appeared on her front step in Billings.

"Ellen?" a slim woman in her late 20s inquired. "I'm Carole Neff, your trainer. And this is Meko."

Ellen's heart sank. Sitting in the doorway was a small black, brown and white mongrel, wispy-haired and droopy-eared.

"Meko might not look like much," Carole said, noting Ellen's dismay, "but she's bright, and six months of training have gone into her. This afternoon you'll get acquainted. Tomorrow we'll start teaching her the locations of important sounds in your house."

That night, Ellen lay in bed thinking, *What have I gotten myself into?* She looked at Meko, who was gazing at her from the other side of the bed. *My life is a dead end. Turning it around is probably too tall an order for a scruffy little mutt.*

The next morning when Ellen awoke, Meko was snuggled beside her, head to head on the same pillow.

"Meko!" Hearing a voice at the front door, followed by the doorbell, Meko leaped against Ellen's knees and ran to the doorway, looking back for Ellen to follow. Carole was at the front door.

"Now praise her, give her love," Carole said, stepping inside.

"Good dog!" Ellen murmured halfheartedly, petting Meko's moist muzzle. Tail wagging, Meko took Ellen's gift of a tiny teddy bear and strutted off. Their training had begun.

Gradually Meko would come to learn Ellen's life: the telephone, alarm clock, microwave timer, teakettle whistle, oven buzzer, smoke alarm. Each sound alerted the dog to get Ellen.

"What do you think of her?" Carole asked Ellen the second day.

"She's so . . . short-haired," Ellen replied, still resisting the little dog.

Carole paused a moment, smiling. "Give yourself a chance, Ellen," she said gently.

On the third day, Carole announced, "You and Meko have to learn how to work together in public. We're going out to lunch."

Ellen felt a rush of fear. "We can't," she insisted. "Dogs aren't allowed in restaurants."

"Not true," Carole assured her. "Certified hearing dogs are admitted. Just show this card. It lists your dog's rights."

Ellen tensed up. She hated confrontation. It only called attention to her deafness.

When the three walked into the restaurant, Ellen had to fight back tears. Swallowing hard, she held out the card to the hostess, who showed the two women to a table. Meko promptly went to sleep at Ellen's feet.

"There," Carole said. "The worst is over."

"No, it isn't," Ellen blurted. "Look. Everyone's talking about us." Only later did she begin to relax.

That evening, after Carole returned to her motel, Ellen took Meko for a walk. She felt confused, uncertain. Did she really want Meko? No, she wanted a dog that didn't need to have daily exercise and that didn't make a fool of her in public. Then she remembered Carole's advice: "Give yourself a chance, Ellen." *Yourself.* Not Meko.

Ellen looked around. She hadn't walked this far in years. The fresh air felt good, and she was in less pain. This little mutt, she decided, had already accomplished something. Or rather, Ellen realized, *she* had done it, with Meko's help.

Hearing-ear dogs, Ellen discovered, were new to Montana. One day while she was walking in the park, an official ran up to her.

"Don't you see the signs?" he sputtered. "No dogs permitted!"

Trembling, Ellen stood her ground. "This is a hearing-ear dog, and state law allows us to be together in public parks." She showed the man her card and the cleanup bag she carried.

"Look," the official said grudgingly, "you can walk around the park, but not inside."

Ellen was even more determined now. "Meko and I are going to enjoy the birds and flowers," she said, surprised by her even tone. "Here's our address. If your superior wants to talk about this, we'll be glad to go in and see him."

The man stalked away in a huff, and Ellen and Meko continued on their way.

A few months later, Meko suddenly vanished. Ellen searched the house, then walked to the park and back, hoping Meko might have slipped away to take their daily walk alone. Finally she went out to her car to drive to the city pound. That's when she realized she hadn't looked in the garage.

As she swung open the door, a small blur of fur shot out and slammed against her knees, bowling her over in the gravel. Ellen saw where paint had been gouged from the door, as the dog fought vainly to answer her calls. She pulled the warm bundle close. "I love you, Meko," she whispered softly. "What would we do without each other?"

Over the years they've been together, Meko has learned her job well. One winter night, Ellen was doing laundry when Meko raced up to her frantically. Ellen hurried after the dog — into a billowing pall of smoke. A portable heater had set a bed on fire, and the smoke alarm hadn't gone off yet.

Today Ellen Raines is totally deaf. But with Meko at her side, she works as a volunteer computer operator. And after losing 50 pounds

For we walk by faith, not by sight.

2 CORINTHIANS 5

84

exercising with Meko, she has resumed social dancing. "My friends say I actually dance better than I ever did," she says. "I don't try to lead anymore. I follow my partner." She strokes the small, sleeping figure at her feet. "Meko taught me that. And a lot of other things, as well."

The best remedy for those who are afraid,
lonely or unhappy is to go outside, somewhere
where they can be quite alone with the heavens,
nature and God.... I firmly believe that nature
brings solace in all troubles.

ANNE FRANK

THE DAY WE BECAME BROTHERS

BY

ALBERT DiBARTOLOMEO

I was ten years old when my father died. Eight months later my mother, believing I needed more structure and male role models, enrolled me in the Milton Hershey School in Hershey, Pa.

A knot in my stomach grew tighter as our car approached the school that February day in 1964. I told myself over and over, *Be brave. Be the man you're supposed to be now that your father is dead.* Actually, I had little idea how to be a man, except to act stoically. So I never uttered a word of protest, though every fiber of my body resisted the trip. *What was my life going to be like? How would the other boys react to me?*

When we arrived, my mother and I were given a tour of the spotless ranch-style house, which accommodated the 16 boys in my unit, with an apartment for our houseparents. My mother remained behind while I was shown the bedroom I would share with another boy.

I returned to an empty living room. "Where's my mom?" I asked.

"Oh, she left," someone said.

Left? My legs went limp. The school's counselor, I learned later, had urged my mother to slip away without saying good-bye so as to avoid a scene.

I spent the afternoon sitting in my new bedroom. When the boys returned from school at four o'clock, they came to look at me. "Boy, you're short," said one kid.

"Lee, he's not short. He's tiny."

"Let's call him 'Ant,'" Lee said.

"No, 'Bug' is better."

"I like those extra eyes he's got," said another, pointing to my glasses. "Maybe we should call him 'Bug Eyes.'"

With that, they went about their after-school chores.

After dinner, we were allowed an hour of free time until study period. I picked up a book and started reading, but my roommate, Jim, interrupted: "There's some things you should know if you don't want to be laughed at. Somebody might ask you to go get a bucket of steam or a left-handed wrench. Your toothbrush will sometimes disappear. Oh, and you'd better keep those glasses in sight all the time."

"Thanks for the warning."

He shrugged. "You'll also probably have to fight somebody soon if you don't want to be treated like dirt."

I sat quietly for a while, absorbing what Jim had told me. Suddenly he asked, "It was your father who died, right?"

"Yes."

He looked into his book. "Nobody's going to want to hear about that."

That night I did my best not to cry. I failed.

Jim's predictions turned out to be true. I got into a fight after two boys played catch with my glasses. Angry, I rammed my head into the stomach of one and we began to slug each other.

I never mentioned my father to anyone, and no one mentioned their lost parents to me. The unspoken code that Hershey boys held was not just the denial of feeling, but the denial that our dead parents had existed at all.

One of the favorite games among the boys was tackle. A football was thrown into the air, and whoever caught it tried to run directly through the rest without being brought down. Tackle was less of a game than an excuse to deliberately smash our bodies into each other for the main purpose, I realized later, of dissipating our frustration and anger.

Late that first spring, Mr. and Mrs. Carney became our new house-parents, and loosened the reins on us. Soon, however, chores were not being done well, and some boys spoke to the Carneys rudely.

Mr. Carney's response was to hold a meeting in which the boys could air their beefs and the Carneys could express their expectations of us. To me, the Carneys were not the "enemy" but surrogate parents who genuinely cared about us. During the meeting I pointed out, "If anything, the Carneys are too nice. Some of you guys are taking advantage of that."

Cold shoulders promptly turned my way. As if to relieve me from the others, the Carneys took me that Friday evening to their weekend house, where I spent most of the time fishing.

When I returned to the unit, Jim notified me, "Everybody thinks you kissed up to the Carneys. You have a lot of guys mad at you."

Great. I had spent months trying to fit in, and in a minute I had ostracized myself. I was not surprised to find my toothbrush in the toilet the next morning.

Two months later I overheard Lee, Bruce and Jim trying to decide how to pass a long August afternoon. "Let's go down to the pond," Jim suggested.

"I say we go to the hide-out," said Lee, referring to a mysterious place I had not yet seen.

"Why don't we just hike," Bruce offered, "and see where we wind up?"

"I'll go for that," Jim said.

"Me too," I added.

"Who invited you, twerp?" Lee said to me.

"Don't call me that."

"Okay, Four Eyes."

Wanting to avoid another fight, I swallowed my anger.

"I'm heading that-a-way," Bruce said, motioning to the open spaces. "If anybody wants to come, fine. If not—adios." He started off, and Jim and Lee followed. I lingered briefly, then joined the group.

After crossing meadows dotted with wildflowers, we found a thin stream. Jumping over it we soon came to a cornfield that stretched as far as we could see. "Let's go in," Lee said, and without hesitation we did.

We quickly became hidden, but pushed deeper into the field. The broad leaves slashed at our faces, and the ears of corn clunked us in the head. We crossed perhaps 30 rows before we halted and sat on the ground.

"Is this the hide-out?" I asked.

"Hardly," Lee said, removing cigarettes from his pants.

"I don't think you should smoke in here," Jim said.

"Me neither," Bruce added.

Lee shrugged. "All right, no sweat." This surprised me, but I soon learned there was something about the cornfield that changed our usual behavior. It was a place that melted inhibitions and tough-guy exteriors. Here, hidden from the world, we found ourselves on those roads into our interiors that we traveled only in private.

Bruce was the first to talk. "My father was a salesman," he said, "and one day a truck ran a stoplight and smashed into his car. He died right there. I was in school, and they called me home. I knew something big had happened but I never thought it was that."

"Mine died of a heart attack," Jim said. "But I hardly knew him. I was four. He was a schoolteacher."

After a pause Lee said, "My old man was a carpenter. He made me a boxcar one summer. He took me to a couple of Yankees games, and once we went to the circus. Then he got bone cancer. He was a big man, but by the time he died, he was like a string bean." Lee's eyes had become wet. He looked away into the depths of the cornfield.

The others did too. They were wearing expressions I had never seen before. No one spoke for a long time. All I heard was the rustling of the cornstalks and the cry of a distant crow.

Bruce broke our silence. "You didn't tell us about your father," he said to me.

I wasn't sure I wanted to. I had survived Hershey by remaining "strong," and I now felt reluctant to allow myself to weaken. But like them, I was eager to unburden myself of something I simply couldn't keep bottled up any longer.

"Mine had diabetes for a long time," I said haltingly, "but it was his kidneys that went bad, and that's what killed him. My mother was called away by the hospital one night. I was in bed when I heard the door open and her footsteps coming up the stairs. They sounded ... sad, so I knew before she said, 'Your father passed away.' "

We didn't talk much about how we felt when our fathers died; we could tell from our faces. Instead we talked about our fathers' lives. What they were like. Who they were. If we'd had pictures, we would have shared them. But none of us had a photo, not even in our rooms, it being generally accepted that such a thing was too much of a reminder of a life more bright and normal than the one we now lived.

The talk about our fathers gave way to other, less weighty matters, and soon we were back to a lighter mood. But when we stepped out into the sunlight, we did so with a common understanding—that life handed out its losses, but we did not have to suffer them alone. For the first

> *Earth has no sorrow that*
>
> *Heaven cannot heal.*
>
> THOMAS MORE

time we realized that we held in common not only parental loss but also the need to release the sorrow that came with it.

As we made our way home, we stopped to drink at the stream. Jim was next to me, and I watched him remove his baseball hat, splash his face and rub his wet fingers through his hair. Then instead of putting the cap back on his own head, he reached over and placed it on mine. The others gathered around, and together we jumped over the stream. And I knew as we returned to the unit that we walked as brothers.

HOW LOVE HEALS

BY

DEAN ORNISH, M.D.

"I ask virtually every patient I see," says Dr. Harvey Zarren, a cardiologist in Lynn, Mass., " 'With whom do you share your feelings?' They look at me like I'm from outer space. But when people feel loved, things happen in their body's physiology that encourage healing. It's just amazing to watch."

My work with cardiac patients over the past 20 years has convinced me that love and intimacy are at the root of health and illness. If a new drug had the same impact, virtually every doctor in the country would be recommending it for his patients. It would be malpractice not to prescribe it. Yet with few exceptions we doctors don't learn much in our medical training about the healing power of love.

It may be hard to believe that something as simple as talking with friends, feeling close to your parents or sharing thoughts openly can make such a powerful difference in your health. But many studies document that these things do.

Scientists at the University of California, Berkeley, studied 119 men and 40 women who were undergoing coronary angiography. Those who felt the most loved and supported had substantially less blockage in the arteries of their hearts.

Similarly, researchers in Israel studied more than 8500 men with no prior history of angina (chest pain). Men who had high levels of anxiety were more than twice as likely to develop angina during the next five years.

However, those who answered "yes" to the question "Does your wife show you her love?" were significantly less likely to develop angina. "The wife's love and support is an important balancing factor," concluded the researchers.

In Sweden more than 17,000 men and women between the ages of 29 and 74 were studied for six years. Those who were the most isolated had almost four times the risk of dying prematurely.

In another study in Sweden, this one of elderly men, those who had low emotional support or who lived alone had more than double the premature-death rate of the other men, even after controlling for risk factors that influence disease.

The power of social support also was seen in the North Karelia Project in Finland. It found that over five to nine years, men who were the most socially isolated had a risk of death two to three times higher than those with the most social connections. Again, these results were found even after adjustment for other risk factors.

Can social ties with friends, family, work and community protect against infectious diseases? To test this idea, Sheldon Cohen of Carnegie Mellon University in Pennsylvania and his colleagues from the University of Pittsburgh and the University of Virginia recruited 276 healthy volunteers ranging in age from 18 to 55. The volunteers were given nasal drops containing one of two types of rhinovirus, which causes the common cold.

Almost all who were exposed to the viruses were infected by them, but not everyone who was infected developed cold symptoms.

According to the study, the diversity of one's social relationships played a powerful role in predicting who would develop a cold.

I believe the evidence is compelling: love and intimacy lead to greater health and healing, while loneliness and isolation predispose one to suffering, disease and premature death.

Why these factors are so important, however, remains a bit of a mystery. I find it extraordinary that such an important and well-documented health factor is not better understood.

"There's a factor here that's difficult to measure," says Dr. Rachel Naomi Remen, clinical professor of medicine at the University of California, San Francisco. "Why do some people get well even though their physicians think they have no chance, while others die who seem to have had every chance to recover? Survival seems to depend on something more than just having the right treatment. Perhaps knowing that others care, that you matter to other people, strengthens a deep impulse toward life—a will to live—that is in every one of us."

I have no intention of diminishing the power of diet and exercise or even drugs and surgery. But scientific studies have made it clear that the capacity to nurture and be nurtured—to have what I call an open heart—is vitally important to having a long, healthy life.

It is only the souls that do not love that go empty in this world.

ROBERT HUGH BENSON

"DEAR SUPERMAN"

BY

DANA REEVE

On May 27, 1995, our life was, in an instant, inexplicably changed. It happened at a few minutes past three, when my husband, Christopher Reeve, fell from his horse as it jumped over a fence. Chris was paralyzed from the chest down and unable to breathe. As he was thrown from his horse, we as a family left an existence of privilege and ease and entered into a life of disability, with all its accompanying restrictions and challenges. We went from the "haves" to the "have-nots." Or so we thought.

What we had yet to discover were all the gifts that come out of sharing hardship. We came to learn that something wonderful could happen amid terrible tragedy.

All over the world people began to respond to Chris's injury. The sheer bulk of mail was astonishing. By our third week at the University of Virginia Medical Center, it was estimated that 35,000 pieces of mail had been processed for my husband.

As a family we opened letter after letter. They provided solace and became a source of strength for me. I used them to elevate my mood or to fortify my spirit to face another day. I could go to the pile of letters marked

"Funny" if I needed a laugh, or to the "Injuries" box to find advice from people in wheelchairs or on ventilators living happy, fulfilled lives.

There were times when I tried to explain the importance of the letters to friends or colleagues, but I could tell they didn't really get it. You had to see it. These letters, I realized, had to be shared.

And so I offer them up to you.

Dear Mr. Reeve,

I just called information for the zip code to Charlottesville Hospital and the operator immediately laughed and said, "Is this for Chris Reeve?" They are getting so many calls.

It must be so wonderful to know and learn how many people are caring about and praying for you. We will get you well; that is a promise.

God Bless You,
Felicia Woodville,
Redondo Beach, Calif.

Dear Mr. Reeve,

The rosary I have enclosed was given to me when I was in the hospital recovering from a car accident. I had just turned 12 and the doctors were not sure if I would ever walk again. The drunk driver who hit me caused severe damage to the right side of my body, as well as my skull. I was very scared and alone.

That was when you walked into my life—or, I should say, flew. My parents brought in a VCR and two of your Superman movies. I can't really say just how many times I watched those movies, but each time they gave me something—someone to believe in. I didn't have to be afraid anymore because, as long as you were a click away, I was never alone.

Today I am a college student who enjoys hiking and tennis, and believes in miracles. I have followed your career for the last ten years and have grown to admire all your work, on-screen and off. The hero I found in Superman then is still the strong, kind person I believe in today. Healing takes a great deal of time, and it's during that process that we discover we are much stronger than we ever imagined.

I just want you to know that you do make a difference! And you will always have a friend in Grand Island. I will keep praying for you.

Very truly yours,
Susan A. Szczublewski,
Grand Island, N.Y.

Dear Chris,

This is the umpteenth letter I have started to you. I just can't seem to get it right. I keep thinking of you, and your family at your side. You are a constant in my memories.

A snow day doesn't go by that I don't remember all the chocolate-chip cookies we made in Mom's kitchen. You would play some ditty on the piano while they were baking.

When my older son plays baseball, I recall the thousands of games in your back yard. Weren't you the one who hit the ball through the window of the garage behind your yard?

Remember how we walked in the snow at night, those summer evenings we spent sitting on the mailbox, or the bubble-gum-chewing contests on Pam's front lawn? We used to laugh all the time and told the stupidest jokes. My sister Deborah (remember you named her "Dead-bird"?) read in the newspaper this morning that you still have your sense of humor. I would expect nothing less.

Every time I see fireworks I am reminded of one Fourth of July. Dad let us set off firecrackers on the terrace. You were barefoot and almost stepped back onto one. We were so invincible then.

We had such a great childhood. I drive down the road and get weepy thinking of what is happening to you now, and I send up a javelin prayer that you can feel God's presence and find his peace in this.

Love,
Louisa B. Huntington,
Hopewell Township, N.J.

Dear Mr. Reeve,
    Six years ago the last thing I used my legs for was to hit my brakes. From that night my life changed so much I didn't think I could do it. I received letters like this in the hospital and hated the people who tried to tell me that everything was going to be okay.

    I was in the prime of life—29 years old. I owned two restaurants, had the best cars, a big house, all the toys.

    And in a split second all that was useless. I went to therapy every day for a year, and swore I would beat this. But every injury is different, and mine didn't turn out to be a success story. I cried and cried till one day I couldn't cry anymore, and I started to live with it. It's not easy. I still have some bad days, but I found out one thing that most people don't know—I found how to be a whole person.

    I am writing this letter to let you know that it's guys like you and me who have to keep our chins up, to help not only those with disabilities but—even more so—people who are not disabled, so they realize just how good they have it.

    There is a happy ending to my story. My two kids have their father with them and I take time to let them know how much I love them, instead of running around like a crazy man all day. Life for me and my wife has gotten more special than ever. I know God will make sense of all this in your mind one day. Until then, work hard at therapy, and be strong. It will get better.

Your friend,
Mark Khayat,
Wadsworth, Ill.

Dear Mr. Reeve,

About 12 years ago my best friend's son, John Beebe, died of cancer of the spine on Long Island. He was 18 years old. His dying wish was to spend some time with you, and somehow word was passed on to you. In spite of your busy schedule, you managed to spend several hours visiting John and helping to make his final days a little happier.

You have had a special place in the hearts of my entire family ever since.

It is heartening to know that your condition is improving a little each day. I am sure that if a generous nature counts for anything in the scheme of things, you will be well very soon.

Sincerely,
Bruce L. Follmer,
Alexandria, Va.

Dear Mr. Reeve,

We shook hands once in 1988 when you were visiting my pediatric patients at Memorial Sloan-Kettering Cancer Center in New York. I will never forget the way you took the time to don hat, mask, gown, gloves and booties to see the children receiving bone-marrow transplants. As you may be aware, many celebrities visit, but none of the TV stars or rap musicians took the time or had the courage to "gown up" and face these unfortunate children. Even though cancer is not contagious, most of the celebrities would not touch them.

All of the children you visited remembered your gentle touch. To them, your heroism was the action in the movies, but to me your kindness and quiet courage was more heroic than any physical stunt performed by Superman.

I wish I could gather those children and come visit you to repay the kindness. I am sure that they are with you in spirit. Recovery from an accident such as yours is a slow process, and it is easy to be overwhelmed and hopeless. One of my patients once told me, "I can't give up—I don't know what fun I might miss."

Rest comfortably, and know that you have had a positive impact on many small lives and at least one pediatrician.

With kindest wishes,
Bruce Reidenberg, M.D.,
Upper Montclair, N.J.

Dear Christopher,

My husband and I were so sorry to hear of your riding accident last week. We understand you are receiving the best medical care available and no doubt the presence of your family and friends is giving you the strength to face this difficult challenge. Individuals everywhere are praying for you and we are among those who are keeping you close.

You may know that Ronnie shares your love of horses. Riding has been a part of his life for as long as I can remember, and nothing could ever keep him from it. He's always felt a certain freedom when he rides—freedom to think and bathe in the silence of the outdoors. I suppose you could say that riding has been nourishment for his body and soul. No doubt you've derived similar joy from the experience over the years, and it is those sweet memories that we pray will carry you through this ordeal.

Please know that you are not alone in this, Christopher. The Lord is beside you, and your admirers are earnestly praying that you will be healed so you might one day resume the active life you were destined to live. God bless you, from both of us.

Sincerely,
Nancy Reagan

A cheerful heart is a good medicine.

PROVERBS 17

Dear Mr. Christopher Reeve,

You may recall me as the person who introduced you to the Japanese participants of the Women's Federation for World Peace (WFWP) International Friendship Conference. In a special expression of their love, the Japanese women of the WFWP hand-made 1000 origami cranes, which is a symbol of hope for complete recovery from illness. I would like to tell you the story of how this tradition began.

A patient who was a victim of the atomic bomb in Hiroshima had to take medicine for the radiation sickness. This medicine was wrapped in small white squares of paper. The patient had to take the medicine once a day. After she finished the medicine, she made an origami crane from each wrapper. It became her wish that each crane would represent another day of life. She began stringing the cranes into long streamers, which she hung from the ceiling, representing her wish for long life. So the doctors told her, "If you finish 1000 rounds of this bitter medicine, you can live." It became her goal to complete 1000 cranes.

This patient inspired a tradition in Japan. When we want to express our deepest wishes for someone's health and long life, we make 1000 cranes. For this reason, we have made 1000 cranes for you, to symbolize your complete recovery and long life. You are always in our prayers. May God be with you and your family.

Sincerely,
Tomiko Duggan and all your friends,
WFWP, Washington, D.C.

Dear Superman,

My sestrs birthday is today. I'm going to invent a poshun that will help you. I'm going to be a jyniour scientise.

Love,
Shane Matthew Morris,
Charlottesville, Va.

It appears that when life is broken by

tragedy God shines through the breach.

GEORGE A. BUTTRICK

TOMMY LASORDA'S "SERMON ON THE MOUND"

BY

OREL HERSHISER WITH JERRY B. JENKINS

My heart sank. The last person I felt like seeing was Los Angeles Dodgers manager Tommy Lasorda. What could he want? Considering my poor performance as a relief pitcher, I wasn't sure I wanted to know.

It was early in 1984, my first full year in the big leagues, and I was hanging on for dear life. I couldn't maintain any consistency. I might get a guy or even two guys out; then I'd get too careful and walk somebody. Tommy hated two-out walks. Almost as much as he hated two-out runs. And two-out runs too often followed my two-out walks.

As a rookie I didn't have that casual relationship with the coaches that the veterans had. I wasn't consulted about strategy. But everyone said I had potential — the most frustrating label any player can have.

Because I was young and looked younger, was thin and wore glasses, was known as a Christian athlete, I often got the feeling that people assumed I had no guts. They called me Howdy Doody or Opie from Mayberry or described me as less menacing than Mister Rogers. Hershiser, they said, was too passive, too nice to get the job done.

I was intimidated by Tommy Lasorda. Loud and brash and a real veteran baseball man, he was a manager any player would want behind him. He could be an encourager, but I didn't know where I stood. There had to be guys in the minor leagues who could do better than I was doing.

And now Lasorda wanted to see me and my pitching coach. What could that mean?

The walk to Tommy's office seemed to take forever. He waved us in. My mouth was dry, and I noticed Tommy wasn't smiling.

"I wanted to talk to you about your game, the use of your ability, your mental approach to pitching," Tommy said.

I nodded.

"You remember how mad I was about how you pitched the other day. . . ."

Did I ever! It was one of those two-out situations with two men on.

"The guy's sittin' on your three-and-one pitch. He knows you can't afford to walk him, and what do you do?"

Tommy was getting himself upset all over again. He grew louder. His face reddened. He leaned closer.

"You laid the ball in for him! Boom! Double and two runs! All because you didn't challenge the guy with a good fastball in the beginning. Hershiser, you're givin' these hitters too much credit. You're tellin' yourself, 'If I throw this ball over the plate, they're gonna hit it outta the park.' That is a negative approach to pitching!"

I knew. I felt small and young and stupid. Sitting there nodding, I thought, *Well, this is what he really thinks of me.* My worst fears had been confirmed. I was hopeless. Tommy was in my face now, those eyes bulging, his cheeks crimson. Sweat broke out on the back of my neck.

"You don't *believe* in yourself. You're *scared* to pitch in the big leagues. Who do you think these hitters are — Babe Ruth? You've got good stuff. If you didn't, I wouldn't have brought you up from the minors. Quit bein' so careful! Go after the hitter!"

As he went on, something registered with me. Had a compliment slipped by, disguised as a tongue-lashing? I've got good stuff? He believes that?

"I've seen guys come and go, son, and you've got it! So go out there and do it on the mound! Take charge. Make 'em hit your best stuff. Be aggressive. Be a bulldog. That's gonna be your new name: Bulldog. You know, when we bring you in in the ninth to face Dale Murphy and he hears, 'Now pitching, Orel Hershiser,' man, he can't wait till you get there! But if he hears, 'Now pitching, *Bulldog* Hershiser,' he's thinkin', *Oh, no, who's that?* Murphy's gonna be scared to death!"

We're nose to nose now, but I don't even swallow. "I want you, starting today, to believe you are the best pitcher in baseball. I want you to look at that hitter and say, 'There's no way you can ever hit me.' You gotta believe that you can get anybody out who walks up there. You're better than these guys."

Lasorda was right. I believed that big-league hitters had special ability. Which they did. What Tommy was telling me was that so did I. I wasn't some minor-leaguer who'd lucked his way up. I belonged on that mound.

No question I had not learned a proper approach to pitching. But I resented anyone's thinking I needed a nickname to make me tough and aggressive.

Two days after our talk, the Dodgers needed a relief pitcher against the San Francisco Giants. I volunteered, despite a tender elbow and an arm weak from overwork. I strode to the mound, reminding myself that Tommy believed in me, thought I was special, thought I would be successful with an adjustment in my approach.

I didn't know what I could do with my arm in bad shape, but my attitude was finally right.

From the dugout, Tommy hollered, "C'mon, Bulldog! You can do it, Bulldog! You're my man, Bulldog!"

I challenged the hitters, kept the ball low, got ahead in the count on nearly every batter. With my arm feeling like a rag, I gave up only one run.

Tommy's talk had made me a believer. If I could do that when my arm felt terrible, think what I could do when I felt great. That day, I became a big-league pitcher.

The "sermon on the mound," as Tommy later called it, gave me the boost I needed to realize my full potential, free of self-doubt and fear. And even if you don't have to face a Darryl Strawberry or an Andre Dawson for a living, the same principle applies: you're good enough to win — whatever league you're in.

Fear knocked at the door. Faith answered.
No one was there.

(on the front of the ancient mantel)

HIND'S HEAD HOTEL,

BRAY, ENGLAND

EDUCATING DAVE

B Y

PETER MICHELMORE

One afternoon in the fall of 1993, Dave Blair, 17, was again cutting English class, heading out the door of Rutherford B. Hayes High School in Delaware, Ohio.

Dave didn't like school, and it showed. As a consequence, his teachers didn't always like Dave. They accused him of "acting out." Maybe he was, but Dave didn't care.

The dark-haired youth was outgoing and popular with his peers, but felt lost in the classroom. He was a slow reader, and when he stumbled over a passage, he sensed the teachers' disgust. "School's got nothing for me," he'd say. "I think I'll drop out." He hesitated only because he'd disappoint his divorced mother, who worked three jobs to pay the bills.

Now outside school, Dave saw a friend approaching a trailer parked in the back since August. "What goes on in the trailer?" he asked.

"I'll show you," the boy said.

In a spacious area eight teenagers sat at a scattering of tables. "Here's someone to help you," Dave's friend said, introducing him to

Sue Scott, a chestnut-haired woman in her early 30s who stood in front of the group.

Dave wasn't sure what to make of the strange kids. Obviously it was a classroom for children with disabilities—youngsters with autism, cerebral palsy, mental retardation. One rattled off a few loud, incoherent words, but most remained silent.

Gesturing to a broad-shouldered youth with narrow, slanted eyes, Sue Scott said, "This is Frank Howard. He'll take you around."

Grinning shyly, Frank, a 20-year-old with Down syndrome, led Dave from one kid to another as the teacher called out their names. Neither Frank nor Dave said a word. "This is our fun time," Sue Scott explained, ignoring the surprise on Dave's face. "We're playing a dice game called Yahtzee."

Dave watched the kids rattle and spill the dice. At first he felt sorry for them. But as they got the knack of it, he saw their faces brighten. Soon Dave joined in the game himself. "Way to go, Frank," he yelled when the youth rolled three aces.

"Hey, I liked that," Dave said to himself as he returned to his classes. "Maybe I'll go back for another visit."

Dave found out that Frank Howard was part of an experimental effort to assimilate disabled children into Hayes High. And teacher Sue Scott, he learned, had developed a program called Club SPORT—an acronym for Supporting Possibilities Opportunities and the Rights of Teens—designed to bring typical kids together with the disabled as advocates, mentors and friends.

To Sue Scott's delight, Dave reappeared at her trailer the next afternoon. When he came in the door, Frank Howard bounded to his side. "Hi," Frank said eagerly.

The two sat together while Sue Scott and some volunteers demonstrated sign language. Each time Frank got a sign right, Dave nodded and Frank flashed a huge smile.

One day Frank met Dave at the door with a look of pride in his eyes. Frank had said very little to him, but now he seemed on the verge of uttering something. Finally it came out. "Dave," he said, softly but clearly. That simple sound, his name, moved Dave in a way that surprised him.

Dave soon sensed that he could be useful in Sue Scott's classroom. She was focused on capabilities, not disabilities. This struck a chord with him. He knew what it was like to struggle. He also saw how Frank was always eager to learn even though everything was difficult for him. Dave's visits to the trailer became a daily routine.

Frank's warmth and joyful spirit drew out Dave's own sense of fun. Clowning around one day, Dave mimicked the stern face of a teacher and ordered Frank to stop fooling around. Knowing it was an act, Frank went into a hip-swinging mime of Elvis Presley that had Dave hooting with laughter.

Later when puzzled friends asked why he hung out with Frank, Dave would say, "We've got more in common than differences." In a note to Sue Scott, Frank's mother Donna Howard wrote, "My son is having the time of his life."

It wasn't all play, however. Using photos of road signs, Dave helped Frank recognize words like *danger* and *stop.* A picture recipe book helped teach Frank how to cook pancakes. With Dave coaching, Frank also practiced his writing, filled out work sheets and learned to find his classrooms.

In turn, Dave felt needed. During one chemistry class he accidentally burned his hand on molten glass. Midway through the next period, his burn throbbing, he asked the teacher for permission to get an ice pack. "You're putting it on," she chided. "It can't hurt that much."

Stung by the rebuke, Dave stormed out. He was still angry when he stomped into the trailer. "That's it for me," he said to Sue Scott. "I'm quitting school."

Then his gaze went to Frank, who was beckoning. Slowly the hurt drained from Dave. He couldn't just walk out. There'd be no more feeling sorry for himself, he decided, no more talk about leaving school. "What's going on, Big Frank?" he finally said, walking over.

Through the winter and spring of 1994, Dave helped ease the integration of the disabled kids into student life. One boy started taking regular math classes; others took home economics, woodworking and physical education. For the most part the kids were accepted.

One day while shopping with her son, Donna Howard saw a group of teenagers coming toward them. "Hey, Frank," they called out warmly.

"Are you students from Hayes High?" Donna Howard asked.

"Yeah, that's where we met Frank," a boy replied. Donna soon got an inkling why they were so friendly. "Hey, Frank, say hello to Dave," one said as they walked on.

At a picnic to mark the end of the school year, she noticed the closeness between her son and Dave. "Dave's helped Frank be all that he can be," Sue Scott told her. "And Frank's enabled Dave to shine when he most needed it."

Instinctively Donna trusted Dave and thought how great it would be if Frank had a night out with his friend. She thought of the four tickets she'd bought for a rock concert, two of which were for her daughter, Aimee, and a friend.

Gathering up her courage, Donna asked Dave, "Would you take my son to an Aerosmith concert?"

Kindness has converted more people than zeal, science, or eloquence.

MOTHER TERESA

115

"I'd be happy to," Dave replied.

In the amphitheater Frank bounced to the beat of the music and plucked an imaginary guitar, his eyes full of excitement. Afterward in the crush of people, Dave was determined not to lose his pal. Aimee spied them coming down the steps. "Dave doesn't care what people think," she said to her friend. "He's holding Frank's hand."

When Dave took a job working nights and weekends at a restaurant, he found a way to include Frank. A nonprofit organization had a program of job tryouts for people with disabilities. The organization agreed to coach Frank for a dishwashing job at the restaurant. Dave had his own ideas.

Club SPORT members stopping in for a meal were delighted to see Frank busing tables. "I want him out with people," Dave told them.

But long hours in the restaurant compounded Dave's problems at school. "You won't graduate at this rate," his guidance counselor told him during his senior year. "You're in jeopardy of returning in the fall."

Meanwhile, Sue Scott drew up a grade chart that scored her students on attendance, attentiveness, attitude, grooming and friendliness. Frank would get a certificate and graduate with the rest of the class.

When Dave heard the news, he told Sue Scott: "I'm graduating with Frank. There's no way I won't make it." And he studied as never before.

Proudly, on a bright Saturday in June 1995, Dave heard Frank's name called, and he watched as Frank received his certificate. Donna Howard's eyes glistened as she heard the applause and witnessed her son's acceptance. Never had she dreamed that this was possible. Then Dave walked across the stage to receive his diploma. Dave's mother was thrilled that her son had finished school.

At a party afterward, Dave plucked silver neck chains from his pocket, each attached to a three-leaf silver clover. Pulling apart the chains, he gave one to Frank. On one side of each leaf he had inscribed their names and graduation date. On the other it read "Best Friends."

Dave's cheeks were now moist with tears. True, he had gotten his diploma, but he had done something he prized even more. He had made a difference in someone's life. Putting his arms around Frank, he said, "We'll be friends forever."

WHY I TEACH SUNDAY SCHOOL

BY
LINDA CHING SLEDGE

Not long ago I was talking with a friend I seldom see. The moment was so bright and easy that she asked if I had enjoyed any other moment as much that week.

"Certainly. Sunday morning at 9:30."

"Really?" she asked. "How can you be so specific?"

"That's when my Sunday-school class meets."

I could see by her surprise that she had never had the privilege of sitting with a circle of teen-agers on an old shag rug, listening to one vulnerable girl tell the others how it felt to be "ditched" by the crowd — and then being lifted on a tide of pure joy as another young hand reached out, in faith and fellowship, to take hers.

There is no way of measuring that feeling or any of the others that keep me coming back every Sunday morning. The reasons and rewards are simple. I teach Sunday school because of:

The smallest mouse. Remember this fable? A group of mice held a meeting to discuss their terrible problem with a cat who was gobbling up their children. After long deliberation, the mice decided to tie a silver bell around the cat's neck to prevent him from creeping up on them unawares.

There were self-satisfied cheers, until the smallest mouse asked, "But who is going to bell the cat?" No one volunteered.

When a church superintendent asked me to teach Sunday school, I said, "No, I teach college all week, and I need a break on weekends. Besides, I don't know the Bible well enough."

"I understand," she replied. "It's hard. Everybody's working. I don't have teachers for your sons' classes either."

Were Tim and Geoff to go without instruction? I'd assumed someone else would take care of them, but it seemed the other church mice were expecting the same. Now my children were in danger of paying the price of our timidity. So I reconsidered and told the superintendent "Yes" — or in mouse talk, "Give me the bell."

Every mother's need for daughters. I have two sons. Where but in Sunday school could I find a bevy of daughters to love and laugh with? Years ago, I had a class of nine-year-old girls. One glorious spring morning, I brought in a record with a song about dancing for the sheer joy of God. We were studying the Old Testament passage in which Miriam, Moses' sister, danced beside the Red Sea to celebrate the Lord's victory over the troops of Pharaoh.

"I love to dance!" serious little Anne said.

So I turned up the music, and all of us skipped and jumped and boogied around the room. The commotion attracted a host of curious parents. Did we feel naughty? Somewhat. But we were as exuberant as Miriam in her dance of victory, as unashamed as King David dancing before the ark of the Lord.

Sunday school also gave me daughters to cry with when there was grief, and to learn with when they discovered the brittle consequences

of bucking the crowd. Here was the next generation of women, each girl different, each one needing something from me and from God. Headstrong daughters like practical Martha of the Gospels. Shy, spiritual daughters like Mary, Martha's sister, who sat at Jesus' feet. Loyal daughters like Old Testament Ruth. In Sunday school, I can help raise these daughters and cherish them.

A legacy of truths. For the past several years I have been teaching teenagers. These kids are used to being entertained, so I like to keep them off guard with quiz games. Like the host of "Jeopardy!" I might say, "Okay, the topic is famous pairs in history. I'll give you the answer, and you give me the question. 'After she cut his hair, he lost the title Mr. Middle East.' "

"Who are Delilah and Samson?" Scott yells out.

"Good! How about, 'He took a ribbing for her.' "

A pause. Then Perian and Megan shout together, "Who are Adam and Eve?"

If teaching the Bible needs a game to engage the minds of our children, it's worth it. Our culture is a legacy of profound truths embodied and preserved in great works like the Bible.

Without Sunday school, some of our children might never hear the ringing words of Psalm 100: "Know ye that the Lord he is God: it is he that hath made us, and not we ourselves." Or the terse bite of Proverbs: "Whoso loveth instruction loveth knowledge: but he that hateth reproof is brutish." Or the healing assurance of the Beatitudes: "Blessed are they that mourn: for they shall be comforted."

I want these children to know what I mean when I refer to "the dividing of the sea" or "the wisdom of Solomon." If our next generation forgets the faith on which our country was founded, it may end up losing the liberties that were purchased with the blood of heroes and martyrs.

The coffee hour. Forget that the cookies are stale and the coffee is watery. I love the coffee hour after Sunday school because it is loud.

Little kids scoot between the legs of grownups and play hide-and-seek in the stacks of chairs placed along the walls. Teen-agers bang on the piano while the minister makes his announcements. Old and young are not simply mingling; they are sharing a joyous racket.

When I look around my neat, suburban world, I see generations separated by walls within walls. I see children spending their days apart from their parents in child-care centers. I see defiant teen-agers drawn into a culture of their own. I see harried parents shuttling between job, home, supermarket and committee meeting. I see older people clustered in recreation halls, alone with their own activities.

But during coffee hour, old and young become a caring, vital community, a mirror of what we wish we could be if we only had the time.

So please pass the sugar. Hi, Seth, have you put in the new kitchen yet? George, that was a great sermon! Geoff, stop pulling my sleeve and say hello to Mrs. Stocker!

Open hearts. Last spring my Sunday-school teen-agers wrote, produced and performed their own rock opera based on the Book of Acts. Not knowing how hard it would be, we dared to put it on for parents at a potluck supper. It was scary.

Kristy and Amy devised dance steps. Eric electrified us with his guitar riffs. Dong Han confounded everyone by singing on key. Some children who had never stood up before adults did so, and with excitement and conviction sang about uncool things like joy and hope and faith. They were simply affirming in their own idiom the validity of the first songs I had learned in Sunday school as a child. Kids will talk to us — and even sing to us — if we just give them their own forum to say in their own way, "Jesus loves me, this I know."

The memory of David. One day I had an argument with Tim, my "baby," who was 16 and already taller than my husband. He accused me of not giving him "enough rope." So I gave him some rope, resentfully and angrily, and he went off to a local rock concert. While he was away, a neighbor called to say that David, one of Tim's friends, had had an asthma attack while playing football and died. My heart bled for David's parents and for my son.

"After the first death," poet Dylan Thomas wrote, "there is no other." Out of this first encounter with death comes either a lifelong sense of futility or, through faith, a transcendent grace and hope. What would it be for Tim?

I waited up and when Tim came home, I told him the devastating news. I watched the child appear in the young man's eyes. "What is the meaning of it all?" he wanted to know. "Why?"

What could I tell him? Words of my own were insufficient. But I had been taught by what I teach, and the first words that came to me were those of the Apostle Paul, who had conquered his own suffering and doubt with faith, hope and love. " 'For now we see through a glass, darkly,' " I told Tim. But eventually, I promised, all would be clear.

Everything I knew of any worth for a time like this I had learned in Sunday school.

Blessed are those who mourn, for they shall

be comforted.

MATTHEW 5

TOUCH OF LIFE

BY

ANTOINETTE BOSCO

When I was 11 years old, we lived in Albany, N.Y., where my parents rented the top floor of a three-story house. The owners, an older Italian couple, lived in the basement. One of their sons had recently married, and he and his wife lived in the middle flat.

My job that summer was to take care of my three-year-old brother, Joey. There wasn't much to do, so one thing that helped relieve the boredom was spending time with my neighbor on the second floor, a young mother-to-be.

They called her Catuzza, which was Sicilian for "sweet little Catherine." Catuzza was well into her pregnancy, and happy though she was, she was also lonely much of the time. She knew very little English, and during the day she missed her husband a great deal. He was a shoemaker and worked long hours to support his budding family.

Catuzza enjoyed the company that Joey and I provided. My brother had golden curls that she would twine around her fingers. Her smile always made me feel that she was wondering about her own small child, in her womb. Sometimes when the baby kicked, she would let me touch her stomach. Once, when Joey was close by, he too felt the baby kick.

After that summer, my family moved to another part of the city, where Joey and I spent the rest of our childhood. I went on to finish school and become a writer. My brother Joe grew up to join the Army, go to college, establish a career with the New York State Labor Department — and, suddenly, discover at age 35 that he had leukemia. Doctors removed his spleen and, considering the degree of malignancy, didn't give him much hope.

However, Joe was determined to live, and he drew strength from the physician he eventually found — a respected hematologist at St. Peter's Hospital in Albany. This doctor would keep Joe alive until he received the new miracle drug that finally put him into remission: interferon. The doctor's name, Joe told me when I visited him in the hospital, was Frank Lizzi.

"Lizzi?" I asked. "That's a familiar name. When we were small and lived on Irving Street, our landlord was named Lizzi."

Joe knew that from family talk and already had mentioned it to Dr. Lizzi. "In fact," Joe said, "our one-time landlord was Dr. Lizzi's grandfather."

"Was Dr. Lizzi's father a shoemaker and his mother named Catuzza?"

"That's right," Joe answered. "What's more, we're not far apart in age. Dr. Lizzi is just three years younger than I am."

Only then did the realization hit me. The unborn baby who had kicked inside Catuzza all those years before on Irving Street had grown up to be the doctor who saved my brother's life.

Not long ago, I watched Joe and Dr. Lizzi as they participated in a telethon for leukemia research. At one point, however, what I saw was not a doctor and his patient. I saw a golden-haired child, his hand on the tummy of a blushing mother-to-be, and I marveled at the mystery of connections. Never would any of us have imagined that this unborn baby would one day return that touch, carrying with it the same miracle of life itself.

WHAT COMPASSION CAN DO

BY
ARTHUR GORDON

Not long ago I attended a memorial service for a successful business leader. In a subdued atmosphere of mourning, various friends paid tribute to him. Finally, a young man arose. The other speakers had been assured and eloquent, but this one, obviously under great emotional stress, could barely speak at all.

With tears streaming down his face, he told the gathering that when he was just an office boy, the industrialist had noticed him, encouraged him, paid for his education. "For a long time," the young man said, "I was no good to him or anyone else. I just failed and kept on failing. But he never gave up on me. And he never let me give up on myself."

Anyone could support a success, he went on to say, but only a rare and wonderful person could continue to have faith in a failure. Now that person was gone, and he had lost his best friend. When his voice faltered to a halt, people everywhere were weeping, not merely for the leader who was gone but for the unashamed sorrow of the follower. When the service ended, I had the conviction that somehow a tiny part of each one of us had been changed for the better.

126

Later I spoke of this to a friend, a psychiatrist, who also had been there. "Yes," he said thoughtfully, "that's what compassion can do. It's the most healing of all human emotions. If we'd just let it, it could transform the world."

The truth is, this quality of compassion — the word means "suffering with" — *has* been transforming the world. It was the force that abolished slavery and put an end to child labor. It was the power that sent Albert Schweitzer to Africa. Mobilized in the March of Dimes, it conquered polio. Without it there would be no Social Security, no Medicare, no SPCA, no Red Cross. But the most remarkable thing about it is what it can do to — and for — the person who feels it deeply.

Or even for the person who feels it suddenly and momentarily. Years ago, with two other college students, I was vacationing in Spain. In Málaga we stayed in a *pension* that was comfortable enough but strangely somber. The owner had little to say; his wife, a tall, tragic-looking woman, always wore black and never smiled. The friendly maid told us that the *señora* had been a concert pianist, but that two years ago her only child had died. She hadn't touched the enormous grand piano in the *pension's* living room since.

One afternoon we three youngsters visited a wine cellar, where the affable proprietor urged us to sample various vintages. We were not at all reluctant — and sang and danced our way home. Back at the house, full of thoughtless gaiety, one of my friends sat down at the piano, flung back the keyboard cover, and began to play, very badly, while we accompanied him at the top of our lungs.

Suddenly the owner rushed into the room, pleading, "No, you mustn't!" At the same instant the *señora* herself appeared, dark, tragic eyes fixed on us. The music died and for an endless moment all of us were frozen with dismay and embarrassment. Then she saw how miserable we were. She smiled and great warmth and beauty came into her face. She walked to the piano, sat down and began playing magnificent, soaring music that filled the whole house, driving the grief and shadows away. And young though I was, I knew that she was free! Free because she had felt pity for us, and the warmth of compassion had melted the ice around her heart.

Look around and you can see this healing force at work in all sorts of situations. One summer day, hiking with my children through the hills of north Georgia, I came to a cabin clinging to a rocky ledge. Behind a picket fence a white-haired mountain woman was working in her garden. When we stopped to admire her flowers she told us that she lived there all alone. My city-bred youngsters regarded her with wonder. "How," asked one, "do you keep from being lonesome?" "Oh," she said, "if that feeling comes on in the summertime, I take a bunch of flowers to some shut-in. And if it's winter, I go out and feed the birds!" An act of compassion — that was her instinctive antidote for loneliness.

Where does it come from, this capacity to share another's grief or feel another's pain? I remember once asking a wise minister about the most famous of all compassion stories, the parable of the Good Samaritan. What made the Samaritan respond when the other travelers who saw that crumpled figure on the road to Jericho simply "passed by on the other side"?

"I think," the clergyman replied, "that there were three things that made him the way he was. The first was empathy, the projection of one's own consciousness into another being. When the Samaritan saw the bandits' victim lying there, he didn't merely observe him, he became a part of him. This identification was so strong that you might almost say that when he went to help the man, he was helping part of himself.

"The second was courage. The ones who 'passed by on the other side' were afraid, afraid that the robbers might come back. The Samaritan had the courage to push those fears aside, to translate caring into action.

"The third thing I'm sure he had was the *habit* of helping. This was no isolated incident in the Samaritan's life. Through the years he had trained himself to respond affirmatively to other people's needs. How? In the same way that any of us can, not so much be heroic sacrifice as by the endless repetition of small efforts. By going the extra mile — occasionally. By giving someone in trouble a hand — if you can. By taking a fair share of civic responsibilities — when you can manage it. These things may not seem to add up to much. But one day you may look around and discover that to an astonishing degree self has been pushed off its lonely throne and, almost without knowing it, you will have become a Samaritan yourself."

Empathy, courage, the habit of helping: qualities latent in all of us that add up to the deep tenderness we call compassion. If only we'd work harder at developing and strengthening it! Because without this quiet power there would be little hope for tomorrow.

THREE WORDS
THAT HEAL

BY
DIANNE HALES

*T*he parent who never praised but was quick to criticize. The unfair boss who handed out the pink slip. The spouse who was unfaithful. These are people who inflicted hurts on us that may take years to overcome, if we ever do. We hold a grudge. We say the worst things to them—or brood over what we wish we'd said. We want revenge.

Actually, the best way to feel better is the opposite of getting revenge. Saying the words "I forgive you" could be the most powerful thing you'll ever do.

To forgive doesn't mean to give in; it means to let go. "Once you forgive, you are no longer emotionally handcuffed to the person who hurt you," explains Robin Casarjian, author of *Forgiveness: A Bold Choice for a Peaceful Heart,* who managed to forgive the man who raped her. One survivor of emotional abuse in childhood says, "Forgiveness extricates you from someone else's nightmare and allows you to live in a state of grace."

If forgiveness feels so good, why do so many people lug around so much resentment? One reason is that it may compensate for the powerlessness they experienced when they were hurt. "People may feel more in charge when they're filled with anger," points out Mary Grunte, co-author with Jacqui Bishop of *How to Forgive When You Don't Know How.* "But forgiving instills a much greater sense of power. A rabbi who lost his family in the Holocaust told us he forgave because he chose not to bring Hitler with him to America. When you forgive, you reclaim your power to choose. It doesn't matter whether someone deserves forgiveness; you deserve to be free."

Another reason we may withhold forgiveness is it can feel like weakness or capitulation. "Some think forgiving means saying they were wrong and someone else was right," says Bishop. But forgiveness isn't about letting the other person off the hook, adds Grunte. "It's about pulling the knife out of your own gut." It can free the ex-wife who remains bitter toward her former spouse, the worker passed over for promotion, the relative not invited to a wedding.

"In many cases, the other person isn't even aware of your misery," notes Suzanne Simon, co-author with her husband, Sidney, of *Forgiveness: How to Make Peace With Your Past and Get On With Your Life.* "While you are turning yourself inside out with bitterness, the one who hurt you doesn't feel a thing."

Forgiving is good for the body as well as the soul. "Reliving past hurts over and over again is bad for your health," says Dr. Redford Williams, co-author of Anger Kills. "Simply remembering an incident that made a person angry has proved to be stressful for the heart." Negative feelings that cause stress have also been linked to high blood pressure, coronary artery disease and increased susceptibility to other illnesses.

While terrible hurts may take only minutes to inflict, forgiving the perpetrator often requires some time. "Initially you experience negative feelings such as anger, sadness and shame," says Michelle Killough Nelson, assistant professor of psychiatry at the Medical College of

Virginia in Richmond. "Then you try to make sense of what happened or take mitigating circumstances into account."

"Ultimately you learn to see the person who hurt you through new eyes," adds Maureen Burns, author of Forgiveness: A Gift You Give Yourself. "With greater perspective, the hurter becomes one who was flawed, weak, sick or ignorant."

Some people may never reach the final stages of forgiveness. Those hurt in childhood by people they loved and trusted may find the process particularly difficult. Yet, even partial forgiveness can be beneficial.

If you want to move toward a future of forgiving but don't know how to start, follow these suggestions.

Practice on small hurts. Forgiving the slights inflicted by strangers—the clerk who shortchanges you or the driver who cuts you off—prepares you for the tougher task of forgiving major hurts, says Casarjian.

Free yourself of bad feelings. Vent your anger or disappointment with a trusted friend or counselor. "This allows you the strengthening experience of being heard," says Grunte. "You can let go of your feelings without the danger of saying or doing anything you'll regret later."

Adds Nelson, "Anger-releasing strategies, such as punching a pillow, can help. If you aren't so much angry as sad, keep a journal." By all means avoid negative expressions of anger such as driving recklessly, slamming doors or breaking things.

Write a letter to the person who hurt you. Spell out the truth of what happened as you experienced it, without blaming or judging. Use "I" statements: "I feel __. I don't understand __." Describe the impact the person's behavior had on you, and express your desire to hear his or her feelings and get the issue resolved.

Should you mail it? "If there is a chance for good, send it," Burns advises. If the person who caused your hurt is dead, however, or incapable of listening to what you have to say, some counselors suggest burning the letter, a symbolic way of letting anger go up in smoke.

Don't feel confrontation is necessary. In cases of incest, assault and other criminal acts, victims may avoid forgiving the perpetrator because a confrontation isn't safe. In fact, you needn't face that person at all. Forgiveness can occur without anyone else's involvement or awareness. "The people you forgive may never realize they wronged you or never know you forgave them," says Casarjian. "They may be alcoholics who cannot hear what you're trying to say. They may deny everything. What's important is that you let go of your anger."

Listen with empathy. "If you do confront your nemesis, listen silently and then relate back what you're hearing," suggests Dr. Williams. "When you do so, you'll begin to see behavior from another perspective and become more tolerant. That can lead to forgiveness."

Meditate or pray. "To err is human, to forgive divine," wrote poet Alexander Pope. "Turn to your spirituality or faith," suggests Burns. "The act of forgiving may be more than any of us can manage on our own."

Don't think forgiving means forgetting. It doesn't. "We cannot forget hurts, nor should we," says Suzanne Simon. "Those experiences teach us not to be victimized again and about not victimizing others."

Look forward in time. By peering into the future, you can benefit from the perspective time brings without having to wait years to achieve it. Consider the two sisters who bickered over the care of their ailing mother. The sister living close by resented being burdened with her mom's day-to-day care while the distant sister just sent checks. Finally the angry sister asked herself what she really wanted in the long run.

"The answer was 'I want to have a good relationship with my sister.' The only way I could do that," she says, "was to let go of my anger and forgive her." Today they can discuss their mother without exchanging

> *Condemn not, and you will not be condemned; forgive, and you will be forgiven.*
>
> LUKE 6

hurtful words, and the distant sister is more willing to telephone doctors and participate in decision-making.

Forgiveness leads to inner peace. "Once you've forgiven," says Sidney Simon, "you'll laugh more, feel more deeply, become more connected to others." And the good feelings you generate will pave the way to even greater healing.

Forgiveness is the fragrance that a violet

sheds on the heel that has crushed it.

ANONYMOUS

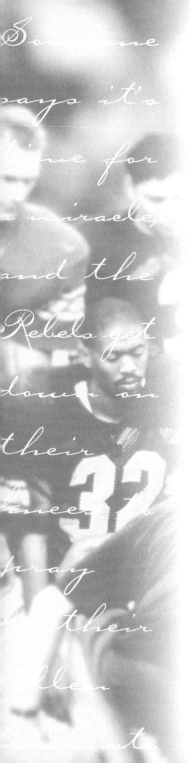

THE POWER OF CHUCKY MULLINS

BY

LAWRENCE ELLIOTT

On a golden afternoon in October, nearly 35,000 fans are watching the University of Mississippi play Tennessee's Vanderbilt University. It is homecoming day at Ole Miss, and the game is scoreless, with 6:57 left in the first quarter.

The Mississippi Rebels have their backs to the goal line; Vanderbilt's quarterback throws to his tailback for what seems a sure touchdown. But Rebel defender Chucky Mullins, a 170-pound sophomore, reads the play perfectly and charges the 208-pound receiver. Mullins hits him helmet-first, bone-hard, jarring the ball from his hands.

Rebel rooters leap to their feet, ecstatic. But all at once the cheers die. For, as other players pick themselves up, Chucky Mullins lies where he has fallen.

Staring up at the blue sky, Chucky thinks, *Give it a minute: it'll come back.* Nothing hurts, but he is having trouble breathing. He wants to loosen his face mask, but he can't. His brain keeps giving the order, but his hands won't answer.

Teammate Chris Mitchell, who has run over to give him a hand up, takes one look and stops in his tracks. Coach Billy Brewer cannot bring himself to move off the sideline.

The trainer kneels beside the downed player, cutting off the face mask. "What's the matter?" he asks.

"I can't feel anything, anywhere," Chucky says softly.

The emergency medical team moves in, immobilizes him on a spine board and speeds him by ambulance to the small community hospital in Oxford. Once doctors there have X-rayed him and seen the catastrophic damage to his spine, a helicopter flies Chucky to the neurosurgery intensive-care unit at Baptist Memorial Hospital in Memphis, Tenn., 75 miles away. He is paralyzed from the neck down and fighting for his life.

Meanwhile, trailing 10-0 at half time, the devastated Ole Miss team runs for the locker room, hoping to hear that Chucky is all right. But all Coach Brewer can tell them is what they already know: if character and courage can make a difference, Chucky has a chance.

Someone says it's time for a miracle, and the Rebels get down on their knees to pray for their fallen teammate. Then, with Chucky in their hearts, they roar back against Vanderbilt, winning 24-16.

He was named Roy Lee Mullins when he was born on July 8, 1969, but never called anything but Chucky. He came from the Alabama town of Russellville, 120 miles east of Ole Miss, where the railroad tracks mostly separated blacks from whites. His mother was a good, hardworking woman who raised three children on her own. Chucky was the youngest.

Carver Phillips, then a coach and playground supervisor, remembers him as a skinny eight-year-old hanging around the park. "He never said much, but he wanted everybody for a friend." Pretty soon Phillips was saving the seat next to him on the bench for Chucky.

In 1981 his mother caught pneumonia and died; she was 32. Twelve-year-old Chucky appeared headed for the orphanage. A few nights after the funeral, however, he telephoned Phillips and, stuttering with anxiety, said he wanted to come live with him. Could he?

A nerve-racking silence followed as Phillips, who was only 25 and had a wife and two babies, absorbed this bombshell. Into the silence, Chucky added, "I'll never give you grief, I promise."

Carver asked his wife, Karen. She said, "Sure."

It was never easy. Karen worked in a sewing-machine factory to make ends meet. Then Carver, employed in a fiberglass plant, fell prey to a crippling lung ailment and was unable to work.

Chucky found a job washing cars at a gas station. One morning, early, the manager sent him to clean the restroom and didn't think about him again until lunch time. Then he went around back, fully expecting to find Chucky asleep. Instead he found him standing tiptoe on a chair, polishing the overhead plumbing pipes. Floor, walls, bowls and mirrors gleamed. "Son, a person could eat off this floor," the stunned manager said. "Why didn't you quit?"

"Quit?" Chucky replied. "Nobody ever told me to quit."

That was Chucky Mullins.

He grew to be a football star at Russellville High School and began dreaming of something beyond the reach of most people he knew: a college education. A football scholarship would be his admission ticket.

The University of Alabama and Auburn University turned him down, saying he was too small and too slow. But Coach Billy Brewer at Ole Miss liked what he saw. Chucky had a feel for the game, a knack for sensing where the ball was going; he had desire and drive.

"I saw a 'glue' player," Brewer said, "a kid who could hold a team together."

Brewer was right. In his first year, it was Chucky who began turning strangers into teammates with his upbeat attitude. When nerves led to a clash of tempers in the locker room, it was usually Chucky who stepped between the antagonists with a joke that got them laughing.

Trea Southerland — given name Thomas Wade Southerland III — a white Mississippian who had gone to a segregated prep school, and Chucky Mullins, a poor black from hardscrabble Alabama, found themselves in adjoining dorm rooms. They had a few chuckles over their wildly disparate backgrounds and promptly became best friends. They ate together, studied together, horsed around together.

That first year was hard, and sometimes Trea wondered if he would ever get playing time. Once, pounding the turf after missing a tackle, he saw Chucky running to help him up.

"Hey, man," Chucky said, "don't fret — you'll get him next time." And Trea thought, *Here's a kid who's had nothing, yet he's worried about me.*

Chucky and Trea made the lineup in their sophomore year, and the Rebels won five of their first seven games. "We are not really that good," Coach Brewer told a reporter before the October 1989 Vanderbilt game, "but we play hard. Sometimes we play over our heads." He pointed to Chucky. "There's one reason."

A chance pregame photo shows Brewer entering the field with his arm around Chucky. There is no hint of the disaster then only minutes away.

Karen and Carver Phillips drive to Memphis, heavy-hearted. They could not love Chucky more if he had been born to them. It is hard to see him with a traction device bolted to his head. "Guess I messed up," he whispers, summoning up a brave smile.

"No, no," Karen assures him. "It'll be okay. You'll see."

"Yeah, right. Maybe no more football." He pauses, and then his eyes meet theirs. "But I'm still going for my degree."

Let us so live that when we come to die even the undertaker will be sorry.

MARK TWAIN

Doctors tell the Phillipses that the force with which Chucky hit the Vanderbilt receiver caused at least four vertebrae to fracture "explosive-ly." Now there is danger his lungs will fail; his condition is critical.

When the swelling subsides, surgeons use wire and a bone graft from Chucky's pelvis to fuse the shattered vertebrae and realign his spine. Neurosurgeon Clarence Watridge tells the press it is the worst such injury he has ever seen. Chucky has borne the operation well, but remains paralyzed from the shoulders down. "The prognosis for return of function is poor," Watridge concludes.

On November 2, Chucky has trouble breathing, and doctors perform an emergency tracheotomy. He remains desperately ill.

But not disheartened. Teammates who visit find Chucky unable to speak because of the opening in his throat; Carver reads his lips. Chucky brushes off questions about himself; he is doing fine. What interests him is how *they* are doing. Are they up for the game against Louisiana State on Saturday?

No one ever hears him complain. Only once, alone with Trea, is he remorseful. He will never be able to repay Carver and Karen for the love they gave him. "I'll just be a burden to them," he says.

Trea grips his friend's hand. "God would not do this to you for no reason, Chucky," he says. "There's more to it, more to come. Don't you know that?" And Chucky nods yes.

Ole Miss officials quickly established a Chucky Mullins Trust Fund and invited contributions from students, alumni and other universities in the Southeast Conference to help meet the staggering medical costs, esti-mated at up to $10,000 a month. They also decided to take up a col-lection at the upcoming Louisiana State game. If there were doubts about how Mississippians would respond to an appeal for a poor black student, they were not voiced.

When a call went out for student volunteers to carry plastic buckets soliciting contributions, the needed 150 were signed up in an hour; hundreds more had to be thanked and sent away.

A record 42,354 people turned out for the game, cheering wildly when the Rebels ran onto the field with Chucky's number, 38, on the side of every player's helmet. The next day, in the bursar's office, the money collected was everywhere — checks in trays; ones, fives, tens and twenties stacked up on chairs and spilling out of fried-chicken buckets. The tally came to $178,168.

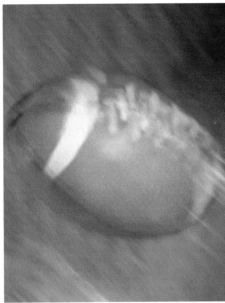

Chucky, allowed to sit up and listen to part of the LSU game on the radio, is stunned to hear the announcers describe the outpouring of affection for him. Soon his story is being told all over America. Money arrives from every state in the nation. By mid-November the total has climbed to $350,000.

Phillips spends hours every day reading letters and get-well cards to Chucky from the bags, boxes and sacks piled up in his room. "It's hard to describe what it meant," Chucky will say, "knowing that all those people were with me."

Later, as the university prepares to elect its "Colonel Rebel," the school's highest accolade, seven standout students, six white, withdraw their candidacies. "It is our hope," they write in a joint letter to the dean, "that all students will show their support by voting for Chucky." It is done.

Is this, the bastion of the Old South, where federal troops were once needed to protect a single black student who wanted to enroll? Can this be the same school where, only the year before, arson destroyed a designated black fraternity house? It is. But now white fraternity brothers wade through the stands, passing the bucket for Chucky Mullins.

On Saturdays Chucky and Carver Phillips watch videotapes of the Ole Miss games together. Chucky nods silent encouragement at the TV. The Rebels, who have adopted the rallying cry "It's time," end the season by defeating arch-rival Mississippi State and gaining a coveted invitation to the Liberty Bowl. Doctors give Chucky permission to attend.

When Phillips pushes his wheelchair into the Rebels' locker room, the jubilant players crowd close, unashamed of their tears. Coach Brewer quiets them and then asks Chucky if he wants to say something to the team. He nods, swallows, gathers strength and whispers into the hush, "It's time."

"I doubt there was a football team anywhere in the country that could have dealt with the Rebels that night," Brewer would later say. Ole Miss sweeps to a 42-29 victory over Air Force.

Come to me, all who labor and are heavy laden, and I will give you rest.

MATTHEW 11

In February 1990, Chucky was moved to Spain Rehabilitation Center in Birmingham, Ala. In July a recurrent bladder infection and related problems required surgery. Still, if there were dark moments, he kept them to himself.

Chucky came home in August, ten months after being hospitalized. Part of the nearly $1 million so far generated by the Chucky Mullins Trust Fund paid for a van and a specially designed house with a wing for Karen and Carver and their children, who were to look after him.

At home games that fall, Chucky sat in a corner of the stands near the players' exit, where each Rebel would clasp his hand and exchange a word. Close observers noted how often Rebel players looked over toward Chucky during games. That season, Ole Miss outgained their opposition by an average 40 yards per game. They kept coming up with the big play when they had to and upset one conference power after another, winning national ranking and an invitation to the Gator Bowl in Jacksonville, Fla.

Against all odds, Chucky returned to classes last January. Some said that was his greatest achievement, but he had an even more breathtaking goal. "I hope to get up out of this wheelchair," he told a reporter. "I know what the doctors say, but I'll never quit trying."

On Wednesday, May 1, 1991, Chucky is getting ready for class when he suddenly stops breathing. A blood clot has shut down his lungs. A nurse attending him immediately begins artificial respiration, and he is rushed to the hospital. But he never regains consciousness and dies five days later.

Afterward some will say it would have been better if he had died right away and been spared the suffering. They do not understand. Chucky, who came here with nothing, has changed the world he lived in. He was, as all America discovered, easy to love.

The entire Rebel team is present when Chucky is laid to rest beside his mother in Russellville. "We came to say good-by," says Chris Mitchell, "but I can't do it. I try, but it won't come. Maybe there are some people you just don't say good-by to."

What lies behind us and what lies before us are small matters compared to what lies within us.

RALPH WALDO EMERSON

MY FATHER'S WAY

BY

GARY ALLEN SLEDGE

*P*ooch was my father's dog, a big, happy, flop-eared mongrel. She wore clown patches of tan and brown on her coat of short, white hair, and was tall enough to meet me nose to wet nose. My father loved Pooch for some improbable promise he saw in her. I saw only trouble.

Pooch was clumsy as an ox and exuberantly affectionate. I had to dodge and weave to avoid her kisses. She outweighed me by ten pounds, and sometimes she knocked me down. As an eight-year-old, I found such behavior unseemly.

That summer it was my job to take care of Pooch, since Dad was away during the week at "the Mountain," his sawmill on 200 acres of redwood and pine above the Russian River on the northern California coast. Mom and I stayed in Antioch in the San Joaquin delta because she didn't want me "growing up lonely and wild in the forest."

Dad wore an old, brown Stetson, and with one side of the oily brim cocked over his eye, he had the sharp, don't-talk-back-to-me look of Humphrey Bogart in *High Sierra*. I was not a little afraid of him.

"You mind your mother," he'd warn me before leaving for the Mountain every Monday morning.

"Yes, sir."

"You water the lawn, hear, every day. Cut it on Wednesday."

"Yes, sir."

"And knock them little almond trees in the back. And Pooch needs good scraps, some of them dog biscuits for her teeth and a good run morning and night." A good run with Pooch was like being dragged by a runaway steamroller.

"You're the man of the house, understand?" I said I did, but I didn't quite see how spending valuable summer hours picking up almonds and feeding his dish-faced, loose-boweled dog meant I was the man of the house.

Pooch always made the most of Dad's leave-takings, dancing around his legs, tail beating like a thick rope against a flagpole in her eager, woeful good-by. Dad would kneel to receive her kisses while he scratched her ears. I thought it was disgusting to be kissed by a sloppy dog.

My father and I regarded each other across a gulf in those days — that awkward, silent space males put between themselves about matters as soul-simple as love and fear. Dad had grown up quick and tough, making his own way in the world, never asking a penny from anyone. He worked his way from Dust Bowl Oklahoma to California, met and married my mother when he was 18 and then was called up to war.

I was born a few months after he shipped out to Saipan, and I grew accustomed to being spoiled by a tight maternal clan of mother, grandmother and a half-dozen aunts. My father's return when I was almost three disrupted that.

In some ways, we failed to live up to one another's expectations. He wanted a rough-and-tumble son who could fish and hunt, while I was a bookworm who wanted a father to hold me in his lap and read to me.

Taking care of Pooch was his attempt to toughen me up and teach me responsibility. I resented the task.

Dad claimed that someday when he had time, he was going to train her. But the one time he took Pooch duck hunting, she came back with her tail drooping and a look of mortal humiliation on her sad-eyed face.

It seemed that at the blast of the shotgun Pooch had hunkered down and begun to whine and shake. Still, Dad did not give up on her. "That dog has ex-cep-tion-al intelligence," he was fond of saying. "All I got to do is teach her discipline and self-control."

Pooch lived in a big doghouse that Dad had built of scrap wood behind a chicken-wire fence in our back yard. I hated going into those dung-marked grounds to feed that dog. Every morning I'd try to sneak in and get her water dish while she was sleeping. Only she was never sleeping. Out she'd jump, tail thumping, foot in the dish, paws on my chest.

Inevitably she'd bound for the gate before I could close it, for Pooch loved freedom more than anything.

Then it was at least a ten-minute chase around the yard. Boy, could she run!

Sometimes Pooch would vault over our five-foot-tall wooden fence, reverse gears and come bouncing back. She'd keep that up — tongue flopping and tail stretched arrow-straight — until she was out of breath. It was hard to have much respect for that dumb dog.

When Dad was home, he looked tired and anxious. I had some hazy idea that money was the problem, and the mill was not making much of it. Late Sunday nights, after a full weekend of work around the house, Mom and Dad would sit at the dining-room table with worried looks on their faces, a stack of yellow bills and a black checkbook in front of them. Monday morning early, Dad would pack up his duffel bag, kiss Mom and start back for the sawmill.

Late in August Dad took Mom and me up to the Mountain for a couple of weeks' vacation. Because there was no way to take Pooch that far in our car, Dad asked one of his hunting buddies, a man with some country-sounding name like Claggert, to care for Pooch.

Claggert's house looked like something out of a Ma and Pa Kettle movie: unpainted, a ramshackle porch, an old car up on blocks, and a bunch of kids running around barefoot. The youngest child was about a year and a half, and there was something wrong with his legs. He lay on the porch in a box while the other kids played around him. I tried not to look at him, yet I couldn't keep from sneaking a glance.

Claggert tied Pooch's leash to a clothesline so she could run, and Dad and I left. It was hard to listen to her sorrowful howling as we drove away.

Unexpectedly, I didn't have a good time on the Mountain. Dad was too busy to take me swimming or fishing, and late at night, lying under heavy quilts, I could hear my parents whisper about "never-end-ing expenses" and the Forest Service demanding "cutbacks" and "fire pre-cautions" and a "chip burner."

During the day, I'd perch on a knobby redwood burl and toss pieces of bark into a bucket. I missed my friends, and I even began to wish that Pooch was with me. At least then I could run up and down the dirt roads with someone, and we could chase squirrels and stalk deer togeth-er. At the end of two weeks, I was ready to go home.

When Dad and I drove back to the Claggerts', the whole family came out on the porch. Mrs. Claggert was holding the baby with the shriveled legs. Mr. Claggert stepped forward with one of his sons about my age. The boy had Pooch on a leash.

"Hi, Bill," Claggert said. He seemed jovial, but his eyes avoided ours. While he traded stories with my dad, I went over and patted Pooch on the head. Her big tail beat the ground, and she licked my hand. But in uncharacteristic fashion she sat politely still, as if they had taught her some manners. The kid holding her gave me a funny look.

"That dog's something," Claggert was saying. "The kids just love her. Smart! Fetch and all. Bobbie here taught Pooch to pull the little one around in a wagon."

"Yeah," Dad said, "be a good hunting dog soon as I get around to learnin' her."

Claggert cleared his throat. "You ever think of selling her, Bill?"

"No, can't say as I have."

"I give you $50 for her."

I gasped. Fifty dollars was an unheard-of amount. Suddenly I was worried that Dad might take it, considering the bad times at the mill. Pooch was part of our family. You don't sell family.

"Nah," my dad said, "she's just a mongrel bitch."

"A hundred bucks."

Where would this dirt-poor Claggert get a hundred dollars? Something was wrong here. I saw a strange expression grow on Dad's face. "I don't want anything for her," he said, flat and hard. "I just want my dog."

"Give her here, Bobbie," Claggert said and shooed his son back to the porch. When my father tried to take the rope, Claggert held on. "I'll fight you for her if I have to, Bill, but I gotta keep this dog."

My father regarded Claggert the way I'd seen him size up a snake that he'd kick or walk around. His hands clenched. "I told you she's not for sale. Period."

"I can't give her to you, Bill," Claggert pleaded. "My wife and kids won't let me." His face was twisted with pain.

"You know my littlest got bad legs. The missus puts him out on a blanket in the front yard there, and the kids are supposed to watch him.

The other day, though, the kids were playing, and the baby crawled out in the road. The missus looks out the kitchen window and sees the baby laying in a rut with a car roaring down on him! She screams. Then Pooch jumps over the fence, runs up and grabs the baby by the seat of his pants and pulls him out of the road. Sure enough, it's some drunk that skids right over where the baby was."

Claggert cleared his throat. "Pooch saved his life."

Claggert looked at my father with pleading eyes. "We love that dog. My wife makes her up a bed in the baby's room every night. We'll take care of her till the day she dies. I'll pay you any amount, Bill."

My father waited in silence, then let go of the leash. "Well, I told you I ain't selling her." He bent down and scratched Pooch behind both ears and ran his hand gently down her smooth muzzle. "So I'll give her to you."

Claggert let out an explosion of breath, took Dad's hand and pumped it up and down. He looked back at his family on the porch and, with a big smile, nodded.

"Come on," Dad said to me, and he started back down the rutted dirt road to the car.

"Why'd you give her away?" I cried, tears springing shamelessly to my eyes. "She's yours!" But I was thinking, *She's mine! I feed and water her. I take her running.*

Dad picked me up and put me on the bumper of the Ford. "Listen, son. There ain't a living thing a man can hold on to in this world unless he loves it and works for it. Those folks love Pooch better than me. By rights she belongs to them."

They don't love her better than me, my heart cried, now that it was too late.

"Come on, be big. I know what you're feeling."

He opened the car door and put me inside, up front with him.

"Yes, sir," I said, coughing back tears.

Let the burden be never so heavy, love makes it light.

ROBERT BURTON

151

Dad got in, started the engine and then did something he rarely did. He put his arm around my shoulder, drew me close and kept me by his side all the way home.

That fall, to support his family, my father finally had to forfeit his timberland and take a job he detested in a pulp mill. But I had learned something important from him — something more important than a lesson in loss. He showed me, in a world marred by misfortune, what effort and sacrifice and generosity it takes to be a man — to hold on to the essential things and to keep safe the ones you love.

Never fear shadows. They simply mean

there's a light shining somewhere nearby.

RUTH E. RENKEL

THE THINGS WE CAN'T CONTROL

BY

DUGAN

The summer I was 13, my father was in a car accident. Though he wasn't injured, it nearly killed him.

My father was my hero—tall, dark, impossibly handsome, perfect white teeth flashing in laughter and song. He had learned to sing from Mario Lanza records, and his clear tenor voice filled the house, the car, the yard, and the forests where the two of us hiked and fished.

Dad and I were often the outdoors duo in our family, while my mother stayed home with my younger sister, Trisha. On weekends we stood by clear streams and watched water spiders skittering on the surface, collected tadpoles in marshes, walked wooded trails gathering animal bones. When I tired or the creeks were rushing, my father lifted me up on his strong shoulders.

Yet, for an outdoorsman, he was a gentle man with a deep respect for all living things—even spiders and bugs in the house, which he caught and released outside. And he was almost obsessively cautious. On family vacations he always drove a few miles *under* the speed limit, which made Trisha and me crazy. In the pre-seat-belt 1950s, he had belts installed in our car and insisted that we wear them.

How ironic, then, that one day a boy on a bicycle turned abruptly in front of my father's car. In a moment the boy's life ended, and my father's life, as it had been, did too.

A laughing, extroverted man, my father became withdrawn. Grief and despair weighted his every thought and movement. Although he consciously knew the accident was not his fault, guilt sat on his soul.

Trisha and I knew an accident had happened, but Dad never spoke of it to us. Our family acted as if the most dramatic thing that had ever happened to us hadn't happened at all. We behaved as if nothing had changed, whereas almost everything had changed.

In 1962, the U.S. Fish and Wildlife Service, Dad's employer, transferred him from the Dakotas. He wrapped things up and flew to Albuquerque to pick up a government car, and Mom, Trisha and I left to visit family.

Dad was a skilled driver. His work demanded travel, and he had driven half a million accident-free miles. He normally found driving relaxing. But the highway was hectic that day, teeming with farm equipment, four-wheel-drive vehicles, tourist buses and trucks. And the car vibrated at Dad's usual speed of a few miles below the 60-m.p.h posted limit. The shudder quieted at 63, however, and after an hour or so he settled into that speed.

As the miles moved under his wheels, he relaxed and enjoyed the striking scenery. He began to sing.

In the afternoon he cleared a mountain range and dropped into a little town at the mouth of a breathtaking valley. The highway was new, smooth and flat, and he seemed to have left all the milling traffic on the other side of the mountain.

Leaving the town, he pulled out to pass an old white-haired man driving at a snail's pace. As he drew abreast, the old man suddenly accelerated, forcing Dad to speed up to finish passing. Noticing his speedometer was over 60, he slowed down. A lone bicyclist pedaled ahead on the shoulder. *Probably a cross-country cyclist,* he thought. *No driveways or turnoffs in sight.* Dad always gave cyclists a wide berth, but he saw that he couldn't now, because an old Army truck was roaring toward him, smoking and clattering. The cyclist, he saw, was only a boy.

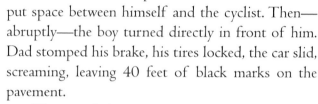

The truck passed and Dad started to pull across the center line to put space between himself and the cyclist. Then—abruptly—the boy turned directly in front of him. Dad stomped his brake, his tires locked, the car slid, screaming, leaving 40 feet of black marks on the pavement.

Where was the boy?

He saw the bicycle's lone front wheel roll into the ditch. When his car finished its long slide, Dad burst out of it, running on trembling legs.

The boy's eyes were already dilated. Dad heard his own voice, high and strained, asking over and over, "Are you hurt, fella? Are you hurt, fella?" The boy was silent and still. He was missing one shoe.

The Army truck backed up and its driver, a tall, sad-eyed man, listened to the boy's chest and thought he heard a heartbeat. My father raced back on shaking legs to his suitcase, spilled it open, and snatched out sweatshirts and his jacket.

With infinite gentleness my father tucked his clothing around the boy. He noticed a spot of blood on the boy's pant leg and slit open the jeans, revealing a fracture. Fatty tissue showed through the wound.

Trained in emergency aid, Dad gripped the boy's leg above the injury to stem bleeding. But the blood had ceased to flow.

"It's too bad," the trucker said. "I don't know how you could have missed him." My father heard these words as from a great distance and stored them away.

He was numb, except for his eyes, which felt as large as silver dollars. As if watching himself, he went to work, moving the bicycle, directing traffic, answering questions.

A deputy sheriff came. He had questions, a camera and measuring tape. "How fast were you driving?" he asked. This question would root itself in my father's soul.

How fast *had* he been driving? He remembered he'd speeded up to pass the old man, then slowed. He hadn't checked his speedometer. He thought he'd slowed to let the clattering truck get past and then begun to accelerate as he pulled over to pass the cyclist. He did not know how fast he'd been driving, and he could not know for sure ... ever. The question became an obsession. Had his speed contributed to the boy's death?

Driving to the courthouse to fill out the accident report, he wondered if he would go to jail. But the sheriff told my father that he was free to go, just stay in touch. That wasn't enough for Dad. He had to speak to the boy's family. So the sheriff drove him to the family's farm.

The farmhouse was filled with people. The boy's mother sat on the sofa weeping with several women, their faces also tear-tracked. The sheriff made a gentle introduction and explained my father's presence.

A curly-haired man, the boy's father, came out of the bathroom. He had been shaving and had cut himself several times. His eyes were wild, but he listened to my father with great control. Dad's voice was high and childish to his own ears as he told the man how sorry he was.

The man insisted that they go to the accident site and re-enact what happened. Jaw clenching, he asked questions, including, "How fast were you going?" As they walked back to the sheriff's car, the man told Dad how much help his son had been with chores and milking their cows.

The ordeal of meeting the family over, now Dad had to tell his wife. *What do you say to your wife?* he wondered. *Will she look at you as a child-killer? Will she still love you?*

He placed the call, his throat so tight he could hardly push words through it, hardly respond to her assurances of love. Afterward, he stood in the phone booth trying to breathe. The pressure inside him seemed to be squeezing his heart and lungs to a standstill.

The day had faded to evening, the weather to foreboding before my father stopped at a motel. There, all alone, he contemplated suicide. By turns he sat numbly on the bed or paced in despair. His life seemed as useless as dust. He felt he would never be even with the world again.

The day after the accident my mother started the 700-mile trip to join him. Before Trisha and I saw Dad again a week later, Mother told us that Dad might seem changed. I remember looking into his face for signs, but my eyes saw nothing different. I was mistaken. My father had embarked on a double life. To his daughters and colleagues he present-ed a face of implacable calm. Yet there were times when this man who hadn't cried since childhood wept secretly in his wife's arms.

And he no longer sang.

Then a peculiar fear began to grow within him. Perhaps, to balance the scales, God might require the life of one of his own children. He had always believed in a loving, fatherly God. Now, unable to comprehend how God could permit this accident, he feared a harsher, vengeful deity.

One day I begged to go fishing with Trisha at the lake across the highway below our new home. Dad debated with himself. A strong wind was blowing three-foot-high waves straight onto the beach. We were good swimmers, but still, Dad hesitated. I begged. Reluctantly, he agreed and struggled to sit at his desk. Yet he rose repeatedly to go to the window. Twice he started for the door to bring us back, but forced himself to sit. He was just beginning to settle into his work when a noise outside snapped him to his feet. Through the window he saw me running toward the house, shouting, panic in my voice, tears on my face.

Instantly he *knew* that Trisha had drowned. He tore out the door, snatching my wrist as he ran toward the lake. From a distance, Dad saw Trisha on the beach, holding my pole and sinker. As he drew closer, he saw the line running to her eye.

Dad put his trembling hands on Trisha's shoulders and murmured comfort and reassurance in a shaking voice. He noted with relief that the hook had penetrated only the flesh below the right eyebrow. He delicately cut the barbed hook out of the small entry wound. Trisha's eye was clear and undamaged.

To err is human, to forgive divine.

ALEXANDER POPE

He held the hook in his fingers with astonishment. Then a smile broke through his emotional imprisonment. For the first time in a long while, he laughed out loud with pure relief. And taking our hands in his, he led us home.

Perhaps Dad's recovery started that day when he saw that God did not exact a compensatory sacrifice for his accident. He began to change—this time for the good. He relocated us back to his beloved Black Hills, to a new house at the mouth of a thickly pined canyon.

Time passed, and once again my father began to feel moments of pleasure. One spring evening almost two years after the accident, I saw him climb the western wall of the canyon, and a while later I heard his powerful voice streaming out of the natural amphitheater in song.

When he came down, I felt that my father had truly returned to me. He was not quite my father of old. He was a man who had passed through a dark fire and survived.

Thirty years after the accident, my father gave me a written account of that terrible time and how it affected his life. Reading it, I wept.

Two years ago, my beloved father lay dying of cancer. He wanted to give me a benediction, to tell me that life is precious but some things lie beyond our control. Yet, even if the horrible happens, God is forgiving. And with that assurance, we can forgive ourselves.

He asked me to tell his story so others would know this too. So I have.

And forgive us our debts, as we also have forgiven our debtors.... For if you forgive men their trespasses, your heavenly Father also will forgive you.

MATTHEW 6

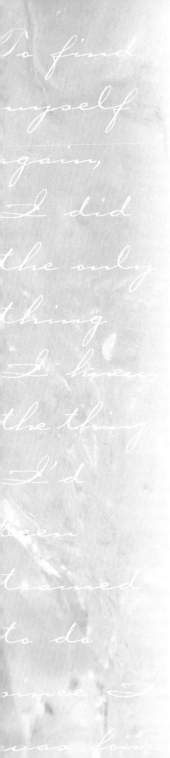

MAKING MY WAY BACK

BY

EKATERINA GORDEEVA WITH E. M. SWIFT

I can see my new life beginning. I glimpsed it for the first time when I was in Moscow two weeks after my husband Sergei's funeral. He had died suddenly of a heart attack during a routine practice in Lake Placid, N.Y. He was only 28.

In my grief I had lost myself. To find myself again, I did the only thing I knew, the thing I'd been trained to do since I was four. I skated. I went onto the ice and there, in the faces of young skaters training with their coaches, I recognized bright dreams and hopes for the future.

I especially feel the stirrings of new life whenever my four-year-old daughter, Daria, is near. No matter how I am feeling, no matter where my mind is wandering, I have to smile back at her because she is always smiling for me. Like her father, she brings the sun into my life.

The spring I turned 11, my coach told me to come early to practice. He had chosen a skating partner for me.

My new partner, Sergei Mikhailovich Grinkov, was tall and handsome and had already caught my eye. But he was four years older and basically ignored me.

For three years we worked together constantly. As pairs skaters, we had to learn everything over again. It is so different from singles skating. Even a simple crossover was different because I now had to do it with someone else and align my body with his.

One day in 1987, when I was 16, Sergei and I were practicing when he caught his blade in a rut in the ice and dropped me. I ended up in the hospital for six days with a concussion.

Sitting in the hospital bed, I was worrying about missing practice when there was a knock on the door. It was Sergei. He was carrying a dozen roses and looked very upset. Sergei visited me several more times before I left the hospital.

When at last I could skate again, I noticed a change in Sergei. He was holding me tighter, as if he didn't want to let me go. Something had happened, and even I—so focused on skating—realized that his feelings for me had changed. Before, we were just two skaters. Now we were really a pair. We went on to win the gold medal at the 1988 Olympics in Calgary, Canada. The following year Sergei and I were married.

Our lives were caught up in competitive skating and then, in 1992, the birth of Daria. In 1994 we won our second Olympic gold medal in Lillehammer, Norway. Soon after, Bob Young, the U.S. Olympic skating coach, approached us about training in the new facility he was managing in Simsbury, Conn. We took him up on his offer and settled in Connecticut.

On November 20, 1995, Sergei and I—along with Marina Zueva, our choreographer—went to a practice session in Lake Placid. We decided to skate our new number, a selection from Grieg's Concerto in A minor.

At the beginning Sergei and I were both on one knee, face to face. Then we started to skate. We did the early movements—a camel spin into a lift. The music softened, and I circled around him.

We did the big lift across the ice. He put me down, and we did a side-by-side double flip. The full orchestra was just coming in, one of those high waves of music. Sergei was gliding on the ice next to me, but his hands didn't move around my waist for the next lift.

He bent over slightly. I thought he had hurt his back. He tried to stop, but I watched him gliding into the boards. Then he bent his knees and lay down on the ice. I kept asking him what was wrong, but there was no answer.

Marina stopped the music and told me to call 911. She started doing CPR. I was so scared I forgot my English. I couldn't remember the word for help. I ran to the other rink, crying, and got someone to call 911. By the time I got back, Sergei was turning blue.

An ambulance arrived. When we got to the hospital, I saw on a monitor that Sergei's heart still seemed to be beating. I was worried but never thought he might die. He had never shown any signs of heart disease.

Marina and I walked around the hospital while we waited. Then a doctor came out and said they had given Sergei electric shocks and a shot of Adrenalin in the heart. But they had lost him. When I translated these words in my head, it was difficult to understand. I didn't want to understand.

I walked into the room where he was lying, still with his skates on. He looked like he was sleeping. His hands were cold, but when I felt his shoulders and chest, they were still warm. I took off his skates. His feet were very cold. I tried rubbing them, but I couldn't make them warm.

I returned to Moscow, where for weeks after the funeral I felt I was slowly losing myself. There didn't seem to be any purpose in life. But my mother said Daria didn't need a sick mom. Whether you live in Moscow or go back to America, she told me, try to be a healthy person again.

I began to realize that work was the only thing that could help me heal. I started practicing again, and it felt good to be touching the ice that was so dear to Sergei. All my memories of being on the ice with him came back, and I found them comforting.

The skating community wanted to hold a tribute to Sergei at the Hartford, Conn., Civic Center in February 1996, and asked me to participate. It was inconceivable for me to skate with another partner— Sergei's was the only hand I had ever held on the ice. I would skate alone to Mahler's Symphony No. 5, music he wrote as a love letter to his future wife.

As the time neared for my solo the day of the performance, I thought about how Sergei and I always kissed before we went out on the ice. It felt terrible to be standing there alone. But as the music started and I skated out into the darkened arena, I thought of what Marina had told me during my last practice: "Just trust Sergei. He will help you."

The lights rose, and I started to skate. The audience began to applaud. I wanted to stop and thank them for coming from all over the world to think of Sergei. But my legs kept moving. I thought, *I can't stop, or I'll lose all this magic and power.* I just listened to my legs. And I listened to Sergei. I'd start a movement, and he seemed to finish it for me. I didn't have a thing in my head. It was all in my heart.

When I had finished, I saw the people standing and clapping. I was handed a microphone. Fighting back tears, I told the audience, "I'm so happy that this evening happened, and I'm sad it's over. But I want you to know that I skated today not alone. I skated with Sergei. It's why I was so good."

On the wings of Time grief flies away.

JEAN DE LA FONTAINE

HOW TO HEAL A
FAMILY FEUD

BY
EDWIN KIESTER, JR.,
AND SALLY VALENTE KIESTER

*T*ears came to Molly's eyes as she looked across the Thanksgiving table at her three sons and their families. Molly felt sad because four faces were missing: those of her youngest son Tom, his wife Eileen and their two children. Years before, Eileen and another of Molly's daughters-in-law had stopped speaking after an incident they resolutely refused to explain. Now they refused even to be under the same roof.

Two years after David's first wife died, he decided to marry again. He asked his oldest son, Charles, to serve as best man. Charles accepted, but then, after a squabble over his father's cat, he suddenly backed out and would not even attend the wedding. Deeply hurt, David cut off all contact with his son. It was ten years later before the two reconciled.

With families more mobile and dispersed than they used to be and their ties fragmenting, virtually every family seems to have some ongoing feud. Often the anger rages for years, painfully wounding other family members, like Molly, as much as the combatants.

Unfortunately, most feuds arise from petty incidents, the details of which are long forgotten, says Jay Folberg, law-school dean at the University of San Francisco and mediator of family disputes. All that remains is a set-in-concrete attitude by parties too stubborn to take a conciliatory step. "I'd make up in a minute," one of Molly's daughters-in-law told her. "But I won't call her first."

In these cases, it may be time for a go-between. This could be a respected family member, a spiritual adviser, a counselor — or you. "Despite the animosity and the duration of the rift," says Folberg, "it's an odd person who doesn't ultimately want a better relationship with people he or she once loved."

If you'd like to bring harmony back to your feuding family, here are some strategies experts suggest:

Do it now. When you see hostilities escalating, step in quickly. The longer you wait, the more embittered participants become, and the harder it is to make peace.

"Remember the clock is always running," says Carl Zlatchin, a psychologist with the California Mediation Service. Bernice Itkin, a San Francisco family counselor who has negotiated numerous deathbed reconciliations, recalls a mother who had bitterly denounced her son after he married someone of a different religion. Years had passed since the two had spoken; the woman had never seen her grandchildren.

Finally, when the mother had only days to live, the son relented. Tears cascaded down her pillow as she embraced him. "Do you have pictures?" she asked in a quavering voice. Moments later, she saw the faces of her grandchildren for the first time. "She died within a few days," Itkin says. "But I'm sure she died smiling. I just wish all reunions could occur in time."

Don't play favorites. Break the ice with both parties simultaneously, making it clear you are strictly an intermediary. That's what Carolyn and

her brother Harold did after trying to make peace between their mother and aunt for nearly a year. "Harold went to Mom on the same evening I saw Aunt Martha," says Carolyn. "That way, neither could feel we had approached the other first."

According to Zlatchin, "If you talk to one before the other, you give the impression that the two of you are going to beat up on the third. You want to avoid that."

Hear each side with a neutral ear. And don't look for confessions or apologies, says Folberg. "Make it clear it's time to create a new history, not rewrite the old one." Adds Zlatchin: "You can begin by saying, 'I don't know how this started, and I don't care. I just know the whole family is being hurt.' That kind of appeal is hard to resist."

Establish ground rules. Ask each party for suggestions about where to meet and what to discuss. Then compare the two lists. Agreement on minor points, such as who sits where or who speaks first, can foster discussion of larger issues.

Sometimes a traditional family gathering can serve as a meeting ground. Aunt Sally's annual barbecue may help each party edge toward the other in a warm, supportive atmosphere. Don't push the idea too hard, however, if either party balks. Some feuders prefer to attempt reconciliation in private, where they feel less "on display."

Once they're face to face, let each state his case without interruption by the other. Keep the discussion centered on problems and feelings, not personalities. Rule out remarks such as "Sam has always had a mean streak" or "Mary has it in for me because I'm smarter."

Above all, follow the agreed meeting plan to the letter. Any deviation may be seen as favoritism.

Try the "Columbo approach." Itkin named this technique after the ostensibly innocent manner of the TV detective. "Now let me see if I have this straight," you might begin. "At the Christmas party ten years ago, she spilled champagne on your new dress, and you've been angry ever since. Do I have that right?" Says Itkin, "When you put it that way, people often see how foolish they've been to blow an incident way out of proportion."

Recall happy times. When Meredith mediated a longstanding disagreement between her father and brother, she stressed special moments the two had shared. "I said to Dad, 'Remember the Little League game when you were umpiring and called Jimmy out? How he cried, and you comforted him and told him people had to be fair even when it hurt? Jimmy still remembers that.' My dad got teary-eyed. I knew I had crossed the first bridge."

"The message," says Zlatchin, "is that good times in the past can mean good times in the future. You have to try to bring back old close feelings."

Don't expect miracles. Some warring parties may agree to let bygones be bygones. For others, the reunion may never be complete. "Mother and Aunt Martha seemed relieved when their feud ended," Carolyn recalls, "although I doubt they'll ever be close again. But it certainly improved my relationship with both of them."

Once the healing process has begun, work to keep it going. A reconciliation of family members not only frees combatants from the baggage of old grudges but also benefits the entire family. And it is those ties of blood — in times of crisis and joy — that give families the strength and support they need.

LILY YEH'S MAGIC VILLAGE

BY

PETER MICHELMORE

It was an awesome sight: scores of costumed children, teens and adults marching through a North Philadelphia neighborhood. It was the annual harvest parade at the Village of Arts and Humanities, an enclave of beauty in one of the city's depressed slum areas.

Thumping on a drum, Lily Yeh, a Chinese-American woman, led the group through streets unlike any others in the area. Sidewalks were swept clean, and old row houses were refreshed. Locust and willow trees shaded parks studded with colorful sculptures. Walls were decorated with splendid murals. Flower and vegetable gardens filled vacant lots. Along the way Yeh greeted residents at their doors with gifts of potatoes, oranges, squash and turnips.

As onlookers watched and applauded that summer day, Yeh couldn't help smiling. "The village was born because of the brokenness of life here," she said. "We didn't run from it. We faced it head-on."

Born in Kweiyang, China, in 1941, Yeh was the daughter of a general in the Army of the Republic of China. Her father kindled in her a love of classical Chinese landscape painting. After moving to the United States in 1963, Yeh earned a master's degree in arts at the University of Pennsylvania. Soon afterward she began teaching at Philadelphia's University of the Arts.

During the 1970s and '80s, Yeh exhibited her paintings and sculptures in galleries. Yet it troubled her that the art world served only a small, prestigious population. She wanted to create art that connected with more people, but didn't know how.

Then one day in the spring of 1985, Yeh was invited to North Philadelphia by a friend, Arthur Hall, who ran a dance troupe from a three-story building in a poor, crime-ridden neighborhood. Hall showed Yeh a weed-choked vacant lot next door. "It looks so ugly," he said. "Do you think you could turn it into a sculpture park?"

Taken aback, Yeh hesitated. The lot was strewn with garbage and surrounded by abandoned houses, boarded-up factories and battered cars. Yet she felt curiously drawn to this neighborhood. To create art in such a place, she thought, was a challenge worthy of a true artist. "Sure I can," she said.

Yeh submitted a proposal to the Pennsylvania Council on the Arts, and in the spring of 1986 she was given $2500 for materials.

Hall asked Joseph "JoJo" Williams, a scrappy middle-aged local handyman, to work with Yeh in transforming the 4000-square-foot area. At first Williams said no. "I'm not helping any Chinese lady build a park," he said. But he relented under Yeh's pressure, and he recruited some 30 children to help.

On the first day Yeh gathered the kids, drew a circle on the ground in the middle of the lot and told them, "Let's work out from here."

By summer's end they'd cleared the area, and Yeh had crafted five seven-foot cement columns on a mound of dirt in the center. She also

painted a ten-foot seascape mural on a facing wall. "We had fun, Miss Lily," a nine-year-old volunteer said. "And it looks so nice now."

Passers-by were less impressed. "It's just a crazy lady and a bunch of kids," Yeh overheard a man tell a companion. "They don't know what they're doing."

Wearily, Yeh packed up her tools and left. But she couldn't get the park out of her mind. She returned the next two summers, directing the kids to plant grass and trees with the help of a local community out-reach program. To add more color, Yeh created mosaics of ceramic tile and glass for her columns. Then she started building more cement pillars.

She hoped neighborhood adults would pitch in, but they avoided her. Then in July 1988 James Maxton, 51, came by. Williams introduced the six-foot-eight-inch, 300-pound Maxton as "Big Man." After watching awhile, Maxton began mixing cement. Later Yeh showed him how to decorate columns with tiles. "Now do a column by yourself," she said.

"Uh-huh," Maxton muttered. Around the effervescent Yeh he was tongue-tied. Unknown to her, he was a cocaine addict who'd trafficked in drugs for 20 years. In his mind, this put a permanent gulf between him and a person like Yeh.

Nonetheless, he stayed on and did four columns in mosaic. "You have a talent for this work," Yeh told him. Maxton felt a glow of pride at her words, but the feeling died with summer's end. Yeh returned to her university job; Maxton continued using and dealing drugs.

Still, something about that summer stayed with Maxton. Over the next few months he vowed, *I'll be back in the spring and I'll be clean.*

It all might have ended there but for a visit Yeh made to China in the spring of 1989. In Beijing she watched students and workers brave-ly marching for democratic reform. In the predawn hours of June 4, Yeh awakened to the roar of tanks and the rattle of rifle fire in Tiananmen

Square. By daylight Chinese soldiers had killed hundreds—perhaps thousands—of demonstrators. In her notebook Yeh wrote, "In doing the right thing, the students did not spare themselves."

Flying back to the United States, Yeh realized the unsparing thing she must do was devote herself to improving life in a Philadelphia slum. Art would be her force for change. The making of art, she believed, brought out the humanity in people.

Yeh decided to formalize her project by creating a non-profit organization called the Village of Arts and Humanities. Her plan was to adopt the neighborhood around the park and turn it into a safe, art-filled village. Since Hall's dance troupe had disbanded, the old three-story building became headquarters.

Hearing about her plan, Maxton presented himself to Yeh. "I was on drugs," he admitted, "but no more. Can I help build your village?"

"Sure you can!" Yeh cried, hugging him.

Winning over Maxton was a big step toward acceptance by the community. Confirmation came one day as Yeh worked on a new mural facing the park, a painting of a mythical bird with a wingspan that spread across the 90-foot wall. "Keep going, girl," a woman who lived in a nearby housing project called out. "It looks terrific."

It is in our power to stretch out our arms and, by doing good in our actions, to seize life and set it in our soul.

ORIGEN

One day while walking along a narrow street behind the building, Yeh paused at a trash-littered lot about 25 feet long. Here thugs often lay in wait to mug passers-by; others came to shoot up drugs. But Yeh saw a different use for the lot. "What a perfect place to make murals!" she cried out to a friend.

With a group of children, she bagged the trash and scrubbed the walls. Her plan was to decorate them with big mosaic angels wearing ornate headdresses and flowing robes. "Pretty little angels with wings won't do," she said. "To protect the children here, we need powerful guardian angels." Soon she began painting the outlines of seven eight-foot angels along each wall. "We'll call this Angel Alley," she told Maxton.

One August afternoon when she'd finished the images, Yeh turned to Maxton and told him, "Go to it, Big Man. You do the mosaics."

For two months Maxton crafted the angels out of mirrors and brightly colored tiles. He was encouraged when people came by to watch and praise his handiwork. "The angels get me out of bed every morning," he told Williams.

A few weeks later Williams strung lights along Angel Alley for a festival. Arriving at dusk, Maxton felt his heart surge with joy. The ceramic gleamed, the mirrors shone like jewels. Tears welled in his eyes. For the first time in his life, he felt worthy.

A year later Yeh was awarded a $50,000 fellowship from The Pew Charitable Trusts in Philadelphia for her park sculptures. She took a two-year leave of absence from the university to pour her energy into the village.

Her target area for the village comprised three blocks containing 79 occupied row houses, 30 abandoned houses and 83 rubble-littered lots. She also began focusing on after-school workshops for children.

Yeh hired a teaching staff and paid a construction crew of five neighborhood men to work with Maxton. They converted vacant lots into a big courtyard inlaid with tile. Other lots were cleared for gardens, where neighborhood residents planted vegetables. One abandoned house was fixed up for offices; another became a crafts workshop; a third became a silk-screen studio. "I never dreamed we'd be able to accomplish all this," Yeh told Maxton.

"It's your dreaming that's making all this work," he said.

One of the participants was Ora Eldridge, who joined the village cleanup crew when she was seven. Some kids teased Ora because her clothes were shabby and soiled. "We don't have running water at home to wash clothes," she explained to Yeh. Soon Yeh also learned that the cupboards at home were frequently bare of food.

Yeh canvassed friends for clothes and told Ora to pick out anything she wanted. Then, figuring other kids might also be hungry, Yeh began bringing fruit and sandwich fixings to the park every morning.

Before long, Ora and about 40 other kids were coming every day after school for tutoring and lessons in art, ceramics, photography, dance and theater. When Ora moved two miles away, she continued to come for dance classes. "I've built my whole life around the village," says Ora, now 17, who plans to study dance and theater in college.

Like Ora, youngsters enjoy the village because it is safe. They don't have to act tough to be accepted there, as they do on the streets. Over the years more and more have been drawn in, including Heidi Warren, a volunteer in 1992 and now the managing director.

In 1995 Yeh resigned her tenured position at the university to devote all her days to the village. Still, she faced distressing hurdles. Williams's health grew poor, and he died of lung cancer.

The next winter the front wall of the main building developed a dangerous buckle. Maxton and the construction crew jacked up the building and reinforced the masonry with the help of Kenneth Williams, on work-release from prison.

Williams, 45, did such a fine job that Yeh hired him as a foreman. In gratitude Williams volunteered to teach classes in carpentry. "Prison is a rite of passage for a lot of young people in the ghetto," he told Yeh. "But it won't be for kids here."

The village has touched the lives of hundreds of children, opening their eyes to a life-style far removed from the mean streets. "You guys don't curse and carry on like other kids," the streetwise Williams told his carpentry class. "You show respect for people. That's great; that's the village way."

Yeh had never preached to the kids about cursing or drugs. "They were part of an old life-style that we've replaced," she says. "Art can have a magical effect on human nature—and that's what happened here."

With the support of a private foundation and the city, Yeh began planning for six new houses last spring. A neighborhood woman recently told her, "We used to walk *around* this area. Now we walk *through* it." Recalling her words, Yeh smiled. It was the best tribute she could hope for.

Good art is nothing but a replica of the

perfection of God and a reflection of His art.

MICHELANGELO

WEED IT AND REAP

BY
SUSAN SARVER

To my eyes my parents' vegetable garden was as big as a soccer field. I'd always imagined this was done to satisfy the perpetual appetites of five children. It wasn't until I married and had two children of my own that I figured out the real purpose of such a large garden. It wasn't the need for more vegetables; it was a need for more weeds.

All five of my parents' children were born "deep feelers." We worried over the most common things. My brothers worried about making the Little League all-star team. My sister wondered whether little Bobby had a crush on her or was just faking nice because she had a new puppy. I worried about whether I was up against the work of Sarah Jane or her mother at the 4-H fair.

My father grew up a farm boy and believed that the only way to flush a worry out into the open was by plenty of sweat. Only the juices of physical labor could lubricate the mind enough to separate life's dilemmas into manageable chunks.

Dad could read signs of trouble on our faces. "The garden needs weedin'," he'd say. "You go out and get started, and I'll be out in a little

180

bit." Sure enough, he'd come and join us just about the time we'd weeded enough to begin talking about whatever was troubling us. As we talked, we'd yank up weeds as though they were conquered fragments of our concerns.

In fact, weeding could whittle away more than worries. A few of us children were prone to quick flares of temper. Pulling up weeds on a hot afternoon was one of the fastest ways to simmer down a streak of fury.

The weeds worked equally well for choking out the bickering and battling that increased immensely during summer months. Mom believed that vegetables eased tensions nearly as well. Picking and shelling a few rows of peas with the enemy was enough to prompt a truce.

Tomatoes were another story. Feuding siblings were never sent to the tomato patch. Put a couple of irascible children there and they were bound to seek out the most rotten, bug-filled tomatoes-turned-weapons—and there was no better target for a mushy tomato than the upturned bottom of a fellow feudling. Mom made this mistake only once.

During the weedless winter, we might have succumbed to the weight of our worries had Dad not come up with able substitutes. In the back yard, for example, he kept a pile of bricks, which he claimed he'd one day form into lampposts. For some reason that brick pile always seemed to be in the way of a growing bush or the basketball hoop.

Quite suspiciously, the mountain of firewood delivered every year faced the same fate. No matter where we stacked it, its placement called for a major shuffle. As we set out to relocate the woodpile, not only did we forget about what had ruffled us in the first place, but a solidarity developed inspired by the injustice of our common sentence.

Eventually Dad grew concerned that our garden's prolific weeds might prove insufficient to match the mounting worries of my two high-school-age brothers, and he began to survey the fields of a nearby

farmer, who had weeds so hardy that they threatened to choke his soy-beans. He was looking for a couple of young weeders to work up and down the rows with machetes.

That conversation elevated the image of weeds, transforming them into the green gold on which my brothers grew rich. Although I begged for a chance to whack my fair share, Mom wouldn't hear of one of her daughters sweating over a machete. So I sat by and watched my brothers' bank accounts grow like the muscles in their arms. Though I envied them, I tried not to show it, as I knew where I'd be headed if my face bore evidence of my feelings.

These days I watch my own children grow increasingly concerned over the dilemmas of childhood. It would help to have a weed patch in which to work their worries over. But as I look at my suburban lot with its too tidy, too mulched, too weedless patch of garden, I know they could barely break enough sweat over it to dilute even a small concern.

So every summer we pack up our worries and haul them 300 miles to my parents' garden. It's the one place in the world where we stand a chance of working out our worries before we run out of weeds.

Though time may heal all wounds, daily
routine provides the bandages.

CHARLOTTE SCHOLL

MESSAGE OF THE POND

BY

PETER MICHELMORE

After their 17-year-old son, Randy, died suddenly from a heart abnormality in 1978, Steve and Mary Shivers moved from the city of Richmond, Va., to a small farm nearby. They kept their jobs — Mary as a high-school attendance counselor, Steve as a filling-station manager — and in their spare hours turned their property into boarding stables for horses.

"The outside of a horse is good for the inside of a man," Mary had said. So it proved. In riding and roping, her husband and older son, Stevie, found release from sorrow. And their robust companionship was healing for Mary too. She took comfort in Steve's belief that God had taken Randy for a special reason.

But all was shattered on December 10, 1984, when Stevie, 24, collapsed in the driveway. Mary watched in horror from the kitchen window while her husband tried to resuscitate their son. "Please, God," he cried, "don't take this boy. I need him."

Death was attributed to acute cardiac arrhythmia, as in Randy's case, but doctors could not explain why the disorder had twice struck strapping boys in the same family.

After months of torment, Steve finally began to recognize that God had not taken his boys to punish him. The world was imperfect, its suffering indiscriminate. Crushed though he was, Steve was only 47 and felt he had to go on with his life and his work.

For Mary, however, there was no relief. "It will change, honey," Steve told her. "One day it will." But Mary could find no solace.

She attended meetings of The Compassionate Friends, Inc., a self-help organization for bereaved parents. Yet she still slipped back into a consuming misery that isolated her from Steve's own determined struggle. To her, he seemed stiff and uncaring.

One year passed, then another. On January 28, 1987, a heavy snowfall had closed school, but Mary took scant pleasure in the sparkle of sunshine on the meadow outside. "My feelings have gone dead," she told Sherri Tolley Arden, 37, leader of the Richmond chapter of Compassionate Friends. With her two daughters, Sherri was visiting Mary that afternoon. "I'll never care for anyone again," Mary told her.

Suddenly Sherri's daughter Brett, 11, bounded up from the pasture and burst into the house. "Lance has fallen into the pond!" Lance was a boarder's 23-year-old appaloosa gelding.

The two women and blacksmith Jim Roberts, 36, who had joined them for coffee, were up and outside in an instant. Slogging through the snow, they reached the frozen pond at the center of the meadow. Forty feet out, Lance's white head bobbed in a patch of dark water. Snorting in fright, he was twisting and straining to find a footing. But the pond was 20 feet deep at that point.

"Get ropes from the barn," Mary told the others. "I'll phone Steve." Steve's instruction was crisp: keep the horse's head above water until he arrived — in 15 or 20 minutes. Mary hung up, then dialed Lance's owner, Patti McFarland.

The rescuers assembled at the pond with ropes and a plywood sheet to distribute weight on the ice. Inching out, Jim tried to lasso the horse's neck, but the panicked animal turned away. The only way to save him would be to go onto the ice and fasten the line to the muzzle ring on Lance's halter.

"Brett will go," Sherri announced. "She's the lightest."

"Yes," Brett insisted, "I can do that."

Mary looked at them in amazement. Six years earlier, Sherri's ten-year-old son, Jason, had drowned. Both mother and daughter had witnessed it. How could they take this risk? "No," Mary said emphatically. "Let the horse die."

Sherri's gaze was locked on the stricken animal. In her mind she saw Jason at Virginia Beach, his surfboard shooting up from a wave behind him, his face contorting as the board cracked the back of his head and sent him under. She had run to him, plunging into water made soupy with swirling sand. But Jason had disappeared, and his body had never been recovered.

"Brett will go," Sherri repeated, as she tied a lifeline to her daughter's belt. The courageous youngster lay on the plywood, and Jim slid her out to the brink. Sherri gripped the lifeline, with daughter Wesley, eight, at her side.

"Here Lance, c'mon Lance," Brett cooed. She saw that his lips were blue from cold and bloodied from ice cuts. She felt a tremor of fear. Fumbling with numb fingers, she needed several attempts to secure latch to halter.

Hauled back safely, she lined up with the others on the rope. Lance was big — 1200 pounds — and the ice was three inches thick. By pulling, they hoped to forge a channel through the ice to the shallows. They were heaving when the catch on the halter snapped and they went sprawling in the snow.

Sherri swiftly grabbed another rope, lay on the plywood and told Jim, "Shoot *me* out this time."

Why, Mary wondered, *is she doing this?*

The ice creaked under Sherri's weight, and she pictured herself falling in under Lance's thrashing hooves. She groped for the halter in the numbing water, made the attachment and signaled to be pulled back.

The horse was weakening now, his breath coming in gasps. The people holding the rope were barely keeping Lance's head above water when Steve arrived.

He backed a tractor to the edge of the pond, attached the rope and began pulling. Lance reared, but his big shoulders hit the ice, and he fell back in the water as the rope broke.

Steve gunned the tractor back to the barn. Returning with a thin, steel cable, he fashioned a loop and sent it whizzing over the ice in an expert lariat throw. Snared at the neck, Lance made another effort to move forward. But he was too exhausted. His shoulders became wedged into a V-shaped gap in the ice, his head sagged and his ears drooped. "This will kill him," Steve said, switching off the tractor.

Looking to the huddle of people, he saw Patti McFarland. She had owned Lance since childhood. More than a pet, he was her best friend. Now the 25-year-old legal secretary had her head on Sherri's shoulder, sobbing.

Watching, Mary felt an outpouring of compassion. An inner voice counseled that they had already put themselves at risk, and Steve would be justified in calling off further rescue attempts. But, fervently now, she wanted the horse to live.

Caution was the last thought in Steve's mind. Twirling a new rope, he looped it over Lance's head and moved to the far side of the hole. With boot heels braced in the ice, he pulled hard to free Lance's shoulders. Suddenly the ice cracked. Steve pitched forward. He felt leaden weights on his legs as his boots filled. *That's all she wrote,* he thought as the water closed over his head.

In one instant, though, his certainty of drowning was replaced by a will to fight. Instinctively he lunged for the horse's tail. Seizing it with both hands, he hauled himself up and around to Lance's neck. Hand-over-hand he pulled himself to firm ice along the cable strung between horse and tractor.

Water spilled from his boot tops, and he was soaked to the skin, yet when he stood, the chill left him. *You're no quitter, man,* he thought.

"I'm getting the mauls!" he yelled. "We'll chop him out."

After Steve returned, he and Jim began hacking at the ice. A big chunk gave way, and Lance struggled forward.

The sight of her husband filled Mary with pride. Aghast when he went into the water, deathly afraid his heart would not take the shock, she had marveled at his run through the snow in water-soaked clothing. *No matter what,* she thought, *he'll keep trying. And I thought this man had no feelings!* Piece by piece, the ice broke, opening a channel. Steve put more tension on the cable until Lance's hooves finally touched bottom.

When the horse was knee-deep, Steve laid down his maul. "Come, Lance," he called warmly. Raising his head, the old horse stumbled onto the hard ice and into Patti's tearful embrace.

After covering Lance with blankets and walking him for three hours to restore body warmth, Steve and Patti dosed the horse with cough syrup and put him in his stall. He would soon recover.

The rescue had been a grueling, hour-long ordeal, yet everyone trooped back to the house feeling that they had shared a wondrous experience. "We sure gave it our best shot," Sherri said. Rarely since Jason's death had she felt such exaltation. As for Steve, he couldn't remember when he last felt so good about himself.

Only when grief finds its work done can God dispense us from it.

HENRI AMIEL

Mary had a sense of being tuned in to a dimension of life that she had forgotten. Warming by the fireplace later, she could contain it no longer. "Did you see what we did?" she said. "Is there a message here?"

That night Mary went over and over the events, and the next morning told Steve, "I know what it meant yesterday. It meant that we *do* care."

And in Mary's gleaming eyes, Steve read the message of the pond. To him, it was the affirmation of a loving God. By giving so profoundly of themselves to save a life, they had discovered a way to renew their own. "Yes, honey, we do care," said Steve. "We always did."

He kissed her, then clamped a Stetson on his graying hair and went out to feed Lance his oats. *It's the breakthrough,* he thought. *Mary's going to make it.*

And at that moment, Steve Shivers felt like singing.

FINDING MY WAY
WITH JESSE

BY

SCOTT RUSSELL SANDERS

On a June morning high in the Rocky Mountains, snowy peaks rose before me. A creek brimful of meltwater roiled along to my left, and to my right an aspen grove shimmered with freshly minted leaves.

With all of that to look at, I gazed instead at my son's broad back as he stalked up the trail. Anger had made him quicken his stride until I could no longer keep up. I had 49 years on my legs, heart and lungs, while Jesse had only 17 on his.

My left foot ached from old bone breaks, and my right knee creaked from recent surgery. Jesse would not slow down unless I asked, and I was in no mood to ask.

The day, our first full one in Rocky Mountain National Park, had started out well. Jesse slept while I sipped coffee and soaked in the early light. We made plans over breakfast without squabbling: walk to Bridal Veil Falls in the morning, raft on the Cache la Poudre River in the afternoon, return to camp and get ready for backpacking the next day.

For the previous year or so, no matter how long our spells of serenity, Jesse and I had kept falling into quarrels. We might be talking about soccer or supper, about car keys or the news, and suddenly our voices would clash like swords.

I had proposed this trip in hopes of discovering the source of that strife. Of course I knew that teenage sons and their fathers always fight, yet I sensed that Jesse was troubled by more than a desire to run his own life, and I was troubled by more than the pain of letting him go.

The peace between us held till we turned back from the waterfall and began discussing where to camp the following night. Jesse wanted to continue up the mountain and pitch our tent on snow. I wanted to stop a thousand feet lower and sleep on dry dirt.

"We're not equipped for snow," I told him.

He loosed a snort of disgust. "I can't believe you're wimping out, Dad."

"I'm just being sensible."

"You're wimping out. I came here to see the back country, and all you want to do is poke around the foothills."

"This isn't wild enough for you?" I waved my arms at the view. "What do you need, avalanches and grizzlies?"

"You always ruin everything." With that, he lengthened his stride and rushed on ahead.

I was still simmering when I caught up with him at the trail head, where he was leaning against our rented car. Having to wait for me to unlock the car no doubt reminded him of another gripe: I had the only set of keys.

The arguments all ran together, playing over and over in my head as we jounced along a rutted gravel road toward the highway. I glanced over at Jesse from time to time, looking for any sign of détente. His eyes were glass.

"So how do I ruin everything?" I asked when I could no longer bear the silence.

He cut me a look, shrugged, then stared back through the windshield. "You're just so out of touch."

"With what?"

"With my whole world. You hate everything that's fun. You hate movies and video games, Jet Skis and malls. You complain that fast food's poisoning our bodies, TV's poisoning our minds and we're all poisoning the earth."

"None of that concerns you?"

"Of course it does. But you make me feel the planet's dying and nothing can be done." Jesse rubbed his eyes. "Maybe you can get along without hope. I can't. I have to believe there's a way we can get out of this mess. Otherwise, what's the point?"

That sounded unfair to me, a caricature of my views, and I thought of many sharp replies. Yet there was truth in what he said. Had I really deprived my son of hope? Was this the source of our strife?

"You're right," I finally told him. "But I don't think we're doomed. It's just that nearly everything I care about is under assault."

"See, that's what I mean. You're so worried about the future you can't *enjoy* anything. We come to these mountains, and you bring the shadows with you. You've got *me* seeing nothing but darkness."

Stunned by the force of his words, I could not speak.

When we arrived at the rendezvous point for river rafting, Jesse and I turned out to be the only customers for the wild 12-mile canyon run. All the others—the reedy kids and puffing parents—were going on the tamer trip.

The water in the Poudre River looked murderous, all spume and suck holes and rips. Every cascade, every jumble of boulders reminded the guides of some disaster, which they rehashed with gusto.

At the launching spot Jesse and I wriggled into our black wet suits, cinched tight the orange flotation vests, buckled on white helmets. The sight of my son in that armor sent a blade of anxiety through me. What if he got hurt? Lord, God, what if he were killed?

We clambered into the raft. Before we hit the first rapids, our guide made us practice synchronizing our strokes as he hollered: "Back paddle! Forward paddle! Stop! Left turn! Right turn!"

The only other command, he explained, was "Jump!" Hearing that, the paddlers on the side away from some looming boulder or snag were to heave themselves *toward* the obstruction, in order to keep the raft from flipping. "I know it sounds crazy," he said, "but it works. And remember: from now on, if you hear fear in my voice, it's real."

Fear was all I felt, a bit for myself and a lot for Jesse, as we struck white water and the raft began to buck. Waves slammed against the bow, spray flew, stones whizzed by. A bridge swelled ahead of us. The guide shouted, "Duck!" and steered us between the pilings and out the other side into more rapids. The raft spun and dipped and leapt with ungainly grace, sliding through narrow flumes, kissing cliffs and bouncing away.

"Forward paddle!" the guide shouted. "Give me all you've got! We're coming to the Widowmaker! Let's hope we come out alive!"

In a lull between rapids, I glanced over at Jesse, and he was beaming. I laughed aloud to see him. When he was little, I could summon that look of delight merely by coming home and calling, "Where's my boy?" In his teenage years the look had become rare, and it hardly ever had anything to do with me.

"Jump!" the guide shouted.

Before I could react, Jesse lunged at me and landed heavily. The raft bulged over a boulder, nearly tipping, then righted itself and plunged on downstream. "Good job!" the guide crowed. "That was a close one."

Jesse scrambled back to his post. "You okay?" he asked.

"Sure, how about you?"

"Great," he said. "Fantastic!"

Hope arouses, as nothing else can arouse, a passion for the possible.

WILLIAM SLOANE COFFIN, JR.

For the remaining two hours of our romp down the Poudre, I kept stealing glances at Jesse, who paddled as though his life truly depended on how hard he pulled. His face shone with joy, and my own joy was kindled from seeing it.

Tired and throbbing, we scarcely spoke during the long drive back to our campground. This time the silence felt easy, like a fullness rather than a void.

That night we left the flap of our tent open so we could lie on our backs and watch the stars. Our heads were so close that I could hear Jesse's breath, even above the *shoosh* of the river, and I could tell that he was nowhere near sleep.

"I feel like I'm still on the water," he said after a spell, "and the raft's bobbing under me and the waves are crashing all around."

"I feel it too."

A great horned owl called. Another answered, setting up a duet across our valley. We listened until they quit.

"You know," said Jesse, "maybe we don't need to sleep on snow. We can pitch camp in the morning on bare ground, then snowshoe up the mountain in the afternoon."

"You wouldn't feel we'd wimped out?"

"Naw," he said. "That's cool."

The stars burned on. The moon climbed. Just when I thought he was asleep, Jesse murmured, "How's that knee?"

"Holding up so far," I told him, surprised by the question.

"Glad to hear it. I don't want to be lugging you out of the mountains."

I lay quietly, following the twin currents of the river and my son's breath. Here were two reasons for rejoicing, two sources of hope. For Jesse's sake, and mine, I would get up the next morning and hunt for more.

REUNION
OF TWO HEARTS

BY
EDIE CLARK

$\mathscr{S}$ix days after my father's funeral, my mother came to live with me. It was not something we would have chosen, but the circumstances were overwhelming. My father had died suddenly, and my mother had cancer and was confined to a wheelchair. She could either live out a shortened life in a New Jersey nursing home, with no family nearby, or she could live with me in New Hampshire.

Often, throughout my 45 years, my mother and I had been at odds. As I was growing up, nothing I did could please her—and nothing she said made sense to me. After I grew up, there had been long periods when we had not spoken. There had been a lot of hurt between us that confounded everyone who knew us.

My mother was a diminutive woman who never seemed to believe that she had grown up. She wore her fawn-colored hair short with bangs to shade her blue eyes. She dressed like a schoolgirl, in plaid kilts and blouses with Peter Pan collars. A lot of people thought this was cute. But when I was growing up, it embarrassed me. I wanted my mother to be more sophisticated, like my friends' mothers.

She was small, and I was big. Before my tenth birthday, I was taller than my mother, who barely reached five feet. This seemed to enrage her. The result was that the battle lines were drawn around food. Perhaps she felt that if I ate less, I wouldn't grow up so fast.

In the mornings she would weigh me on a blue bathroom scale beside her bed. Even a gain of half a pound provoked a scuffle. She apportioned me tiny bits of food, which left me starving. To satisfy my hunger, I squirreled stolen food away under my bed. She would sometimes find this stash and fly into a rage. There were days of silence between us and then days of reconciliation.

Mealtimes were agony for all of us. My father, quiet and reserved, stayed clear of the battlefield. The only thing he insisted on was that I show my mother respect, which I found hard to do. When I left home for college, I returned only for brief visits. I'm sure this hurt her very much.

In 1973 I came to live in New Hampshire, in part to put distance between my mother and me. We kept in touch but saw little of each other.

Yet she kept pictures of me throughout her house. She was proud whenever one of my stories was published. We couldn't be together for long, however, before words grew sharp and tempers short.

Still, my mother found ways to communicate her profound love for me—mostly through phone calls and letters. If we had an argument, she would put it aside and let it blow away. When I got older, it began to dawn on me that my mother had a lot to teach about forgiveness. As I made preparations for her arrival, I vowed to make up for my part in this storm-tossed relationship.

I returned home after Daddy's funeral to prepare my house for Mom. Meanwhile, my sister, Chris, who had flown in from the West Coast, drove her to New Hampshire. I stood in the driveway on that March day in 1994 to welcome them. When she saw me, Mom lifted her hands in delight. Then she waved me away. "Look," she said, and she carefully walked into my house—no cane, no wheelchair to steady her. Her incredible recovery didn't last long, but this was my mother: determined, stubborn, impish and mysterious.

Hospice volunteers came to talk with me before my mother arrived.

In an effort to introduce them to her, I showed them a picture of a beautiful, tiny woman with a radiant smile and the stripes of a corporal on her sleeve. It was taken in 1944, while she was in the Marine Corps. "Your *mother* was a Marine?" everyone responded, incredulous.

"Tell me about the Marines," they would ask. And she would. She sat in her bed and told stories I had not heard in years. She told about the officers who barked in her face and sent fear into her heart. She told about her 99 female roommates and how they all wore pajamas—and how she alone had arrived with lacy nightgowns.

All these years and I had never given much thought to her military service. Now I realized what it must have meant when she stepped up to the recruiting desk, a petite woman who wasn't afraid to go to war.

Our favorite venture together was to go for rides. She liked the back roads that lead to farms and views of Mount Monadnock. We'd set forth, a different direction each time. Mom sat happily in the passenger seat, a blanket on her lap, watching the scenery. "Look," she'd say, pointing to a cluster of blooming yellow daffodils by the road, a childlike delight in her eyes. Sometimes we'd watch the sunset reflect on the lake.

We were both widows. It gave us common ground. She wondered how I had stood it, being alone all this time, and said she worried about me.

She also grieved for Daddy, her lifelong companion. They had known each other since childhood and had rarely been apart except during the war. Something would come up about him, and tears would fall, but her grief was sporadic.

Most of the time she seemed content, even happy. It was often reported to me by hospice volunteers that, when I was not there, she would lean over and in a conspiratorial whisper say, "I think Edie *likes* having me here." And I did.

A lot of our time together, we spent alone. I came home at five to relieve whoever had been with her in the afternoon. The house quiet, I'd pour us each a glass of sherry. She'd hold her glass aloft and make a toast. "To us," she'd say, and we'd clink our glasses.

Then I'd tend to supper. We had made a list when she first came, and all her favorites—chicken and dumplings or corned-beef hash—emerged from my kitchen.

Mom's mobility did not last long. She began to fall, and gradually she made the transition to the wheelchair and finally to bed. Her hands lost strength, and she could no longer write or even hold a fork.

Each phase she bridged gracefully. When she began to spend every day in bed, she continued to come to the table in her wheelchair for meals, but even that fell by the wayside quickly. "I'd like to eat in here," she said one day, while sitting up in her bed. So I tied a bib around her neck and fed her. "We've gone full circle," she said, smiling, the first time I fed her custard.

We were no longer able to take drives, but I would take her out in her wheelchair. To get Mom out of bed, I had to reach my arms around her in a bear hug, and she would put her arms around my neck. When I bent to lift her, she would purse her lips and make smooching sounds, an endearing greeting that harked back to good-nights when I was little. Once she was settled, I tucked blankets about her and trundled her out to the garden, and we'd sit there until she grew chilled. Afterward she would sink back into her bed, exhausted but happy from the excursion.

Many times when we were alone like that, I tried to muster the courage to talk about the past. At last, one Sunday afternoon, it seemed as good a time as any. "Mom," I said, turning to her, "I'm sorry we have had so many difficult times."

She reached over, took my hand and gave it a squeeze. "We're having a good time now, dear. That's all that matters."

Throughout those days I saw not only the mirthful, somewhat eccentric woman who was my mother, but also a sweet and gentle lady who truly cared for others. One day my friend Sandy came to visit. Mom was not feeling well, but when she saw Sandy, she perked up. "Sandy," she said, "you have such beautiful hair."

I was deeply touched by her ability to reach out at that late hour in her life. In a way, I fell in love with her. Did this newness negate all of my experiences with her? Did it make a liar of me, who had always been so angry with her for her need to control everything about me? I don't think so.

Maybe we are destined to walk through some paces before we learn what we need to learn. Later that spring, I thought it deeply ironic that Mom and I became once again locked into the issue of food.

Mom's throat no longer had the strength to channel water into the stomach rather than the lungs. Thick liquids were okay, however, so I made her some cauliflower and cheese soup.

"Here, let me," she said, trying to help me bring a full spoon to her mouth, much more than I would have given her. I didn't resist her attempt to feed herself, but I should have. She took in one mouthful and began to choke. Her face reddened, and then tears streamed down her soft cheeks. Tears streamed down my cheeks as well.

I had been advised by the hospice nurses: if she chokes, don't call an ambulance, because an emergency medical team may perform a tracheotomy and put her in the hospital where feeding tubes would be inserted, which is what we were working to avoid. She wanted to die at home.

At last she stopped gasping and began breathing normally. I held her hand and told her how much that had scared me. She nodded her head. I didn't know what to do if this happened again. Was I supposed to watch her choke to death?

Later I called the hospice and voiced my concerns. "She can no longer be given food or water," they told me. Her ability to swallow anything was virtually gone.

It was heartbreaking to give her nothing. At that point, I called my sister and my aunt and uncle to come to stay. We sat beside Mom, holding her hand, stroking her forehead. We dipped a small sponge in water, wrung it dry and brought moisture to her lips. Sometimes she would bring her tongue out to greet the sponge. Other times she would shake her head, no, no.

For six days we sat in vigil, taking turns holding her hand and stroking her hair. As each day passed, Mom drew further from us. She spoke only our names when we entered the room; then she only blew us tiny kisses; then she only watched, her eyes large and reddened. At last her eyes closed, and her breathing, rapid and shallow and rhythmic, was our only clue she was alive.

On the last day I sat beside Mom and meditated about a bird being released from a cage into blue sky over a field of wildflowers. I leaned close to her. "Fly free, Mom, fly free," I whispered to her.

We witness...by being a community of reconciliation, a forgiving community of the forgiven.

BISHOP DESMOND TUTU

Her breathing geared down, slower and slower. Her eyelids moved and seemed to be opening. Gradually, as if coming out of a deep sleep, her eyes opened, and she looked into mine, a burning gaze. She murmured something, but I couldn't understand what she said. After perhaps a minute, she closed her eyes. Like a clock winding down, she stopped.

We brought chairs into the room and sat at the end of Mom's bed, holding hands, crying. Mother, this slight, tiny, childlike person, far from her disease, looking at peace at last.

The mysteries of my mother will most likely escape me until the day I die. I have no way of understanding why she was the way she was when I was growing up, why we clashed so tragically. Neither do I understand why the lives of my mother and me conjoined for that brief time at the end of her life. I can only voice that I am grateful they did. My mother did indeed have a great deal to teach me about forgiveness. I believe that we only ever get glimpses of the truth, and I did get the briefest flash of this just as the sun was setting, just as she was leaving me, on that evening in May 1994.

The most important trip you may take in life is meeting people halfway.

HENRY BOYE

FAMILY TIES

BY

LINDA CHING SLEDGE

My husband, Gary, and I were flying to Hawaii from New York City to show our five-month-old son, Timmy, to my parents for the first time. But what should have been a mission of joy filled me with apprehension. For five years I'd hardly spoken to my father. Loving but stern in the manner typical of Chinese fathers, he had made particular demands on me, and though we were very much alike, we'd grown very far apart.

When I became a teenager, my father held up my mother as a model of feminine behavior. But she was gregarious and social, while I preferred books to parties. He pressed me to mingle with his friends' children. I insisted on choosing my own companions. He assumed I'd follow in my mother's footsteps and enroll in the local university to study teaching, and that I'd marry into one of the other long-established Chinese clans on the islands and settle down, as he and my mother had.

But I didn't settle. As bullheaded as my father, I escaped to the University of California, where I fell in love with a *haole*, as we called Caucasians from the mainland. Gary had blue *haole* eyes and sandy *haole* hair. I announced that we were getting married—in Berkeley, not

Hawaii. No huge, clamorous clan wedding for me. My parents came and met Gary just two days before our small, simple wedding. Afterward we moved to New York, as far from the islands as we could get without leaving American soil.

My father's subsequent silence resonated with disapproval. He didn't visit; neither did I. When my mother telephoned, he never asked to speak to me, and I never asked for him. We might have gone on like that, the habit of separation hardening into a permanent estrangement. Then Timmy was born, and I felt an unexpected tidal pull back to the islands.

On the long flight to Hawaii, memories of my childhood, when I was my father's small shadow, came flooding back. I was three years old, running behind him as he walked between the banana trees in the plantation town where he taught high school. When I grew tired, he carried me on his shoulders. From there I could see forever. "You are my sunshine, my only sunshine," he would sing. "You make me happy when skies are gray." I laughed, taking his devotion as my due.

Now the prodigal daughter was returning with the firstborn of the next generation—a hazel-eyed, golden-skinned *hapa haole* (half-white) child who looked little like his Chinese ancestors. How would my father react? If he disapproved of Timmy, as he had of me, the breach between us would be complete. I would never return.

The plane landed, and I gratefully placed a crying, hungry Timmy into my mother's eager arms. Here was instant and unconditional acceptance of a child by his grandmother.

My father's expression was passive and hard to read. He greeted us politely: "Good trip?" Then he peered cautiously at Timmy, who promptly began to shriek. My father stepped back in alarm. Did he find it unsettling that this squalling stranger might be his own flesh and blood?

After dinner at my parents' house, Gary and I retired to my old bedroom. My mother tucked Timmy into a borrowed crib in a room down the hall.

Four hours later mother instinct pulled me from sleep. This was the time Timmy usually woke for a bottle, but there were no cries of hunger, no fretful wails. Instead, I heard only the sweet, soft gurgle of baby laughter. I tiptoed down the hall.

In the living room, Timmy lay on a pillow on the floor in a circle of light, his plump, tiny fists and feet churning gleefully. He studied the face bent over him, an Asian face burned dark by the Hawaiian sun, with laugh wrinkles at the corners of the eyes. My father was giving Timmy a bottle, tickling his tummy and crooning softly, "You are my sunshine . . ."

I watched from the darkness, not wanting to break the spell, then crept back to my room. It was then I began to suspect that my father had wanted to mend the breach as much as I had. Awkward and proud, he hadn't known how, and neither had I. Timmy became the bridge over which we could reach for each other.

For the rest of our stay, the tension slowly melted. My father and I didn't discuss our rift directly. Thanks to Timmy, we didn't need to. Having claimed his *hapa haole* grandson, my father no longer defined our family by a uniform set of features. Curly-haired, hazel-eyed Timmy was loved for himself.

We returned to the islands the following summer. Timmy, now a toddler, splashed in the surf with his grandfather. The summer after that, they built a treehouse out of scrap lumber and painted it blue.

So pleased was my father with his new grandfather status that he took early retirement when Timmy was four, to spend more time visiting his "New York family." My son and my father made a handsome pair as they walked together—the Chinese grandfather happily trailed by a different, bouncing shadow.

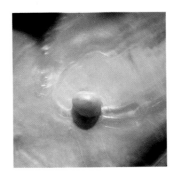

It is the wounded oyster that mends its shell with pearl.

RALPH WALDO EMERSON

MY FATHER, MR. LINCOLN AND ME

BY

EDWARD ZIEGLER

I had a penny from my father, a consolation award for trying to file a nick out of his ax blade. I had failed. And the penny—which in those days could buy two pieces of bubble gum or a little balsa-wood glider—was small consolation. I had hoped for five cents and, in my mind, had it spent—even though I knew I had not persisted in my chore.

Sharpening the ax blade wasn't just an idle task. Dad needed sharp tools to chop kindling for the cookstove. It was 1938, and our family had rented an old farm in Vermont to get away from the sweltering streets of Brooklyn, where Dad was a Methodist minister.

I studied the penny dejectedly. "Don't be discouraged, Teddy," my father said. "I'm sure you did your best." He was giving me more than my due. "Look at your penny, there," he went on. "You know whose picture that is?"

"Yes. Abraham Lincoln."

"That's right. And he had any number of setbacks too. But he didn't stay discouraged."

208

Dad smiled and continued in the style of his "junior sermons." My older brother, Michael, who was eight, sat down on a white-birch stump. I stood nearby.

Dad asked what we knew about Lincoln. All I could offer was that he had been born in a log cabin and used to read by firelight. Michael knew more: Lincoln freed the slaves and saved the Union and was shot for his ideals on the same day that Jesus got killed— Good Friday.

True, said Dad, but did we know that Lincoln ran a grocery store that failed, leaving him deep in debt? That he was unsuccessful in two tries for a Senate seat—in fact, endured a life marked by failure after failure? And yet, few lives had been lived more triumphantly.

"Above all, Lincoln was a man of character," Dad said. "And he had fortitude. That's what you should have right now, Teddy. It means having the strength to bear misfortune calmly and patiently."

Then came a surprise—the sermon's clinching illustration that has lived in my memory ever since.

"Lincoln was a very great man—morally and physically," Dad said. "Why, you know he was six feet, four inches tall!" He went over and plucked a sharp pencil from his back-porch desk, where he worked on his sermons and correspondence. "Come on, boys. I'll show you how tall that is."

He pointed to one of the porch posts. "Teddy, you first." I flattened my six-year-old spine against the post and felt the pencil brush my head as Dad scribed a line indicating my height. Above the line he wrote my initials, "EWZ," and the date. He did the same with Michael, writing "MSZ." Next he marked his own height, five-foot-eight, and wrote "VEZ."

Then, using his folding carpenter's rule, he drew a line far up on the white-painted post, and printed: "A. Lincoln—6 feet 4 inches." At that moment, I imagined I could see Abe Lincoln standing there.

Dad told us more about him: the fun-loving flatboatman, the prodigiously strong rail-splitter, the surveyor, the self-taught lawyer, the orator and finally the brooding President.

The message that came through was that Lincoln's greatness owed much to his constructive use of his setbacks. Failure, Dad said, can teach you far more than success. Enduring adversity, we flourish in new ways. Accepting setbacks, we learn to go forward.

Years went by. As a student of history in high school and college, I learned more about the great man, and came to appreciate my father's particular respect for Lincoln's willingness to get his hands dirty.

"Remember the dignity of physical labor," Dad said. "Believe in the perfectibility of every man—'in the better angels of our nature,'" as Lincoln himself phrased it. "Avoid the abuse of power—'have faith that right makes might,' not the other way around."

More years passed, and I had sons of my own. Following my father's lead, I tried to inculcate Lincoln's values in them.

One August afternoon when the boys were five and seven, my wife and I took them to that old farmhouse in Vermont. The place looked smaller than I remembered. It seemed surprisingly neat. And then it was clear why. It had been recently repainted. As we walked up the driveway, we called out a greeting. There was no answer. The place seemed abandoned. As we got behind the house, I could feel my pulse racing.

At first it was hard to recognize the back porch as the same one that my father had used for his office. Gone were the rough desk and pine shelves he had fashioned nearly 30 years before. But a thought began to insinuate itself into my mind: Would the old marks still be there?

> *Determine that the thing can and shall be done, and then we shall find the way.*
>
> ABRAHAM LINCOLN

A crazy idea—they doubtless had been covered over by the new coat of white enamel. I turned to face the Lincoln post and felt a sudden, quiet fulfillment. It was immediately clear that some stranger had chanced upon our shrine and paid his respects to it. The thoughtful house painter had skipped the side of the post where Dad had concluded his sermon all those years before. The inscriptions were still legible.

We studied them silently for a few moments. I imagined the painter standing there in spattered coveralls, torn between curiosity and the desire to finish his job, looking slowly up the post, as initial succeeded initial—until his gaze took in the topmost inscription. Who can imagine what reeled through his head? Whatever it was, it was close enough to the spirit of the original occasion to stay his hand.

Suddenly, old pictures of my own flashed in my mind. And I had to think how easy that task of filing the ax blade would be today, were I given it once again. From the failure and the sermon I had learned something: that we each have the power to grow, all the time, if we are daring enough. And if we allow ourselves to be imbued with the spirit of a great person, if we can open our minds and keep them open, we will grow inwardly. It had happened with Lincoln. It had happened with my father and me. It would happen with my sons.

"Want to add your initials?" I asked the boys. Matt, the five-year-old, was first, straightening against the post as I traced his height and penciled in "MSZ." Andy was next, a few inches taller. After completing his "ANZ," I stood back to engrave the scene in my mind.

There, visible after all those years, was the penciled legend now towering above the five sets of initials: "A. Lincoln—6 feet 4 inches."

A
HEALING BIRTH

BY

LAWRENCE ELLIOTT

*A*ll day that Saturday in March, the bright two-story house of Mary and Abe Ayala in California's San Gabriel Valley rang with music and laughter, sounds of celebration for their daughter Anissa's sweet-16 party. Relatives and friends came and went. The party spilled out into the garden, warm with the colors and promise of spring.

Anissa was radiant with rosy skin and burnished brown hair, one moment the teen-age coquette, the next wide-eyed as a child, awed by her mountain of birthday presents. She was a sophomore at Walnut High School that year and considered by many students to be among the prettiest and most popular girls in school. She was a solid B+ student, slender and lithe, a soccer player on the girls' team. Monday to Friday, the Ayalas' telephone began ringing for her almost as soon as she got home from school, and it continued through the weekend.

She was the only girl in the family, and her parents adored her. Abe and Mary had grown up 18 miles and a whole world away, in the impoverished barrios of East Los Angeles. The grandchildren of Mexican immigrants, they knew all about hard work; it was that and nothing else that had moved them up from poverty in a single generation. Mary had been a hairdresser for 18 years before taking over as bookkeeper at the repair business for diesel truck instruments Abe started several years after he came home from Vietnam.

Now they lived in suburban Walnut in this handsome house, whose master bedroom was bigger than the homes the two had grown up in. They were committed churchgoers and grateful to God for their blessings, of which the greatest were their two children, Anissa and her 17-year-old brother, Airon.

On that golden day in 1988 when Anissa turned 16, there could not have been a happier girl in Southern California. And as she danced and flirted, she could forget the ache in her left side that had dogged her for a month and the mysterious bruising she'd told no one about.

It had begun with an angry purple bruise on the hip against which she carried her schoolbooks. Other bruises erupted on her legs whenever she made even glancing contact during a soccer game. Anissa thought briefly about telling her mother, but she knew what the reaction would be: "We're going straight to the doctor." And that meant missing soccer practice. So she said nothing.

But there were other symptoms she could not hide. One afternoon Abe was driving her home from a soccer game. "You okay?" he asked.

"Sure. Why?"

Abe had noticed her simply running alongside the girls on the other team, not trying to take the ball away.

Anissa looked away. She *had* been out of breath. And her legs felt as though they were dragging rocks. In the second period there came a time when her head swam and she thought she might faint. Worried the coach would take her out of the game, she had driven herself beyond the limit of her reserves but just short of total exhaustion. Thereafter she tried to pace herself, gearing down when she thought no one was watching.

Then the pain started. First it was a dull ache in her side. Next came a stabbing sensation in the stomach, rousing her out of deep sleep late one evening. From then on it recurred, night after night. She would double up, pressing a pillow into her middle and biting her lip to keep from crying out. Still she said nothing.

On Easter Sunday, one week after Anissa's birthday party, the Ayalas returned from church and sat down to a big family dinner, the table laden with all the Mexican dishes Anissa loved. But after only a few mouthfuls, she began pushing the food around on her plate. Soon her mother said, "You've hardly touched anything. Don't you feel well?"

"I'm okay," she replied, and managed to eat a little more.

But after dinner Mary cornered her daughter in the kitchen. They made a striking pair. Mary was as attractive as her daughter, though a head shorter, and looked more like a sister than her mother. They had always been very close; Anissa often said her mother was her best friend. "All right," Mary demanded, "tell me what's wrong. Have you got a fever?" She put her lips to Anissa's forehead and exclaimed, "You do!"

Unable to avoid Mary's anxious eyes, Anissa could not keep the secret any longer. "I think something's the matter with me, Mom. I feel tired all the time, and I have these pains in my side and my stomach. And look . . ." She lifted her skirt to show ugly bruises on both thighs.

"Oh, my God! What is that?" Mary gasped. Then she caught herself and became the protective mother, seemingly unworried, bent on not frightening her child. Matter-of-factly she said, "Well, whatever it is, we're going to see Dr. Gutierrez about it right after school tomorrow and find out what has to be done."

She brooded about whether to tell Abe. Finally she did, and they tried to reassure each other. But that night Mary lay awake for a long and fretful time, troubled anew over a chapter in their lives she had believed to be closed.

Mary Ayala: When Anissa was 12 she had scoliosis, curvature of the spine. I didn't see it coming on. By the time I realized that one of her shoulders was higher than the other, the orthopedist said it was too late for braces or exercises. She needed major surgery.

It was the worst moment of my life. I said to the doctor, "What kind of mother must you think I am, not to have brought her here before? But I never noticed."

He said that wasn't unusual. Scoliosis advances so gradually that you might not realize anything is wrong until the condition is far advanced, like Anissa's.

But I was just torn with guilt. I couldn't bear to think of them cutting open my little girl's back and fusing her spine to a metal rod. I went all over Southern California looking for a less drastic solution. But wherever I went they all said the same thing: she had to have the operation, and soon, or she would be disabled for life.

Anissa took it without a whimper: the brutal surgery, all the blood transfusions, and the rehabilitation that lasted more than a year. For eight months she wore a metal brace whenever she was out of bed. But when she went back to school the next September, she got right into her old routine, sports and all. Oh, how I thanked God.

And now—those bruises. As soon as I saw them, I thought about all that blood Anissa had been given four years before. Had some of it been contaminated with HIV? Did my daughter have AIDS?

Dr. Frances Gutierrez had been the Ayalas' family doctor from the beginning. She had delivered both Airon and Anissa and seen them through the whole range of childhood illnesses. She was also Abe and Mary's counselor of last resort during the more serious ones. That Monday afternoon, listening to Anissa's symptoms, feeling her enlarged spleen and seeing the ominous bruises, she suspected the diagnosis, but all she said to the Ayalas was that she wanted to do some blood tests.

Inside, the doctor was heartsick. She had been practicing medicine for 24 years and had treated thousands of families. The Ayalas were on her top-ten list of patients—just plain good people. "When I saw what was ahead for Anissa—this sweet child who'd already been through the scoliosis nightmare—I felt angry," she says today. "It seemed so unfair. But God has his reasons, doesn't he?"

Anissa left the office unworried. She had that sense of indestructibility that comes with youth, and she was confident that Dr. Gutierrez would make her well. On the way home she asked her mother to drop her off at the shopping mall; she was meeting friends who would help her decide how to spend some birthday gift certificates.

Mary had been watching Dr. Gutierrez closely and knew something was seriously wrong. And barely an hour after she returned home, her telephone rang. It was Dr. Gutierrez saying she wanted Mary to come back to the office.

"But Anissa's not here," Mary replied weakly.

"I don't want Anissa. I want you—and Abe."

Trying to fight panic, Mary telephoned Abe's shop and told him they had to see Dr. Gutierrez. When he asked her why, she said she didn't know, but she thought it was bad news about Anissa.

Abe Ayala was stunned. While waiting for Mary to pick him up, he went into his tiny office above the shop and tried to collect himself. His mind kept turning to the same devastating thought: *She's going to die.*

Abe felt vulnerable, exposed. It was like the time he was wounded in Vietnam, when someone in his squad tripped a booby trap. And he turned now, as he had then, to God. He was deep in prayer when he heard Mary's car outside.

Abe Ayala: Mary says I'm too cautious. Maybe. When I started this business, we didn't spend a penny on anything but absolute necessities until we had seven months' worth of mortgage payments in the bank. No matter what happened we'd have a place to live.

It was the same with having the kids. We married young but waited five years. I know what it is to be poor; I wanted better for my children. They became more precious to me than my own life.

When we got to Dr. Gutierrez's office, the first thing I saw was that she had tears in her eyes. She asked if we knew what a normal white blood cell count was. We said no. She said it was from 5000 to 10,000 per cubic millimeter; Anissa's cell count was 328,000. That's why her spleen was swollen. That's why she had pain in her left side.

But it wasn't AIDS. "Anissa has leukemia," Dr. Gutierrez said.

For one crazy second I felt hope; it wasn't AIDS! Then I saw Mary's face crumble and it came to me—leukemia. That's the disease children die of.

By the time Anissa got home, Mary was there waiting. She came bursting in, eyes bright with excitement and calling out, "Wait'll you see what I got, Mom!" She perched on the edge of a chair in the family room where Mary was folding clothes. Surrounded by her parcels and bags, she began tearing the wrapping from a pink skirt. "I'm going to wear this to school tomorrow," she said exultantly.

Then she realized that her mother, who could share her joys over a new outfit as giddily as any of her friends, was avoiding Anissa's eyes. "What's the matter, Mom?" Anissa asked.

"You won't be going to school tomorrow," said Mary. "Dr. Gutierrez wants you to have some tests. You'll have to stay at the hospital for a few days."

"Why? What tests? What's the matter with me?"

Mary shook her head. It was a moment before she could trust her voice. "I don't know. But I'm sure it's nothing to worry about."

Anissa left her packages where she had dropped them and went to her room. She knew her mother too well to be fooled. There must be something seriously wrong with her.

Meanwhile, her brother, Airon, had come home. The high-school senior's tall and rugged frame hid a tender heart. He took one look at his mother, reflexively folding clothes but lost in some faraway darkness, and sensed trouble. When he asked her what was wrong, she told him that his sister was very sick: she had leukemia and would need to go to the hospital so doctors could find out what form of the disease she had and whether it was far advanced.

The next day, on the way to Children's Hospital Los Angeles, the usually bubbly Mary sat beside her husband, not saying a word. Anissa was convinced that they knew more than they were telling her. *Why did Daddy take a day off from work if there's nothing to worry about? Why does he keep looking back at me in the rearview mirror?* But then she thought, *If they don't want to talk about it, okay; I'm not going to upset them by bringing it up.*

At the hospital everything was ready for her. As soon as she was settled in bed, a nurse came to draw blood from Anissa's arm. Then there was a doctor and another nurse. They showed her on a doll how they were going to anesthetize her hip so she wouldn't feel anything when they put a needle in and did a bone-marrow aspiration—drawing fluid from her pelvic bone.

When that was finished, Anissa noticed a lot of whispering going on between various doctors and her mother and father outside her room. When they came back in she looked up, hoping somebody would have something to say to her, but nobody did. When she asked her mother to tell her what the doctors said, Mary told her they were waiting for the test results.

Mary and Abe left around 11 p.m., reassuring Anissa that there was nothing to worry about. Then a nurse came in and gave her a pill. When Anissa asked what it was for, the nurse said they were starting her on a course of chemotherapy. Anissa had an instant vision of her cadaverous-looking grandmother in her last days; she had lost all her hair from chemotherapy treatments, then died of cancer.

Anissa handed the pill back. "I'm not taking this," she said. The nurse's eyes went wide. "I'm not taking anything, or letting you do anything else to me, until someone tells me what's the matter with me."

Soon one of the younger doctors who'd been around earlier came into the room. "What's the trouble, Anissa?" he said, as he might to a five-year-old.

Anissa coolly told him she wasn't a child and wanted to know what was going on. "All day the doctors have been having conferences with my parents, but so far no one has told me anything."

The doctor was sitting on the edge of her bed. Only the table lamp was lit; the rest of the room was dark. He said, "I may be jumping the gun, Anissa, but we think you have something called CML—chronic myelogenous leukemia—an adult cancer of the blood."

She felt her heart lurch. *Well, I asked him and he told me.*

The next morning, Anissa awoke determined to fight back, to take charge of her illness. And that's what she told her mother when Mary arrived later that day at the hospital. "No more secret conferences between you and Daddy and the doctors; I have to be in on everything. Okay? If I'm going to die, I want to know why—quit crying, Mom!— and if I'm going to live I certainly need to know what *I'm* supposed to do."

Mary, heart and mind in turmoil, could only nod. And so it was. Starting that day, and in all the ones that followed, Anissa listened, asked questions, pondered what she read in encyclopedias and medical books, and acquired an intimate knowledge of *her* leukemia.

It was, she learned at the outset, the consequence of a genetic change in a single white blood cell somewhere in her bone marrow. For unknown reasons that cell had turned malignant and was reproducing itself. Leukemic cells overwhelm healthy cells, attack the body's blood-producing organs and cause anemia, infection and internal hemorrhages. Without medical intervention, the leukemia can prove fatal in weeks.

Even when brought into remission, relapse and ultimately death are the likeliest outcomes.

Anissa's leukemia, CML, was a chronic form of the disease, which meant that it could only be treated—not cured—by certain anti-cancer drugs. With luck her blood count would improve, the pain and bruising would disappear, and she could live symptom-free for as many as five years.

Even this was more a hope than a prognosis. The mutant cells were tough; inevitably some would survive the chemotherapy and the cells *they* produced would be immune to further chemical attack. In effect, Anissa was living with a time bomb ticking away inside her: the rate of fatality for CML was 100 percent, regardless of the treatment.

She did have one chance, though, that went beyond treatment. It was a relatively new procedure that replaced her sick bone marrow with the marrow cells of a compatible donor—a transplant. The doctors explained that this gave them the possibility of destroying *all* the leukemic cells with a powerful combination of radiation and chemotherapy. But this would also put Anissa's immune system out of commission for as long as 15 days, and for that period her life would hang in the balance. But if her body did not reject the donor marrow, or if, in its defenseless state, it was not beset by a major infection, new cells would begin to multiply and she could have hopes for a cure.

Mary: I don't think Abe or I accepted the reality that Anissa was dying until we finally understood how tough her leukemia was. When they told us about the transplant possibility, we went from the dumps to a kind of wild hope. When they said that siblings were most likely to have compatible white cell patterns, and that Airon had the best chance of being the marrow donor Anissa needed, we were in seventh heaven; we felt maybe we were home free.

But a simple tissue-typing test established that Airon was not a match, which left him crushed and mortified, and shattered our fantasies of a speedy cure. Not knowing what else to do, Abe and I had ourselves tested. Other close relatives volunteered to be typed also, but all the results were negative.

I asked myself: What do we do now? I said to Abe, "Our child is dying." I kept asking the doctors and hospital staff: "What do we do?" Then someone told me about an organization called Life-Savers Foundation of America in Covina, Calif., just a few miles north of our home in Walnut.

Life-Savers, one of the first bone-marrow recruitment centers in the West, had been started in 1988, the same year as Anissa's diagnosis, to find tissue-matching donors for people with leukemia. It went on to sponsor tissue-typing tests for potential donors to be entered into a national registry.

In any given case, the odds against finding a successful match are discouragingly high. But little by little Life-Savers and similar centers across the country had begun improving the odds. That is where things stood on that day in November 1988, when Mary sat in the office of peppery Tami Brown, director of operations for Life-Savers. Mary told her story, ending with what was becoming a constant question: "What do we do now?"

Tami Brown would never forget this first encounter: "I looked across my desk and saw this sort of broken woman, all crumpled in her chair, voice shaky, a little weepy, and I thought: *This lady's not going to make it.*"

But in her most professional manner, she explained that the chance of finding a matching donor for Anissa was one in 20,000, and that in the national registry of potential donors, which covers the entire United States, there were only 17,000 names.

"It's not possible?" Mary whispered.

Tami said it was *possible,* just statistically unlikely. She explained that the best thing Mary could do for Anissa was to encourage more volunteers to be tested for a match.

"She looked at me as though I had two heads," Tami recalls. " 'Me? How?' she asked. So I told her, 'Get on the phone. Put up posters. Organize meetings. You and your family make speeches to the Rotary Club and the Lions Club and the chamber of commerce. Every marrow donor you recruit builds up your daughter's chances. And, oh yes—you have to raise money for the tissue-typing tests. They are not cheap.' "

Mary slumped deeper into her chair. No one in her family had ever spoken in public before. How could they go around asking other people for money? They were hardly paupers.

Tami felt sorry for her. Patiently she spelled it out: The sums they were talking about were not trivial. Each tissue-typing test cost $75, and to have any reasonable chance of finding a match for Anissa, the Ayalas were going to have to bring in potential donors by the thousands. There was no public funding; the only way to get the money was to raise it privately.

But, Tami added, the effort would not be for Anissa alone. Every name added to the registry would become available to each of the 16,000 children and adults who fall ill with a fatal blood disorder every year. Tami said it was too bad it had to be that way, but the families of leukemia victims were the program's best salespeople.

Then she let loose with what she called her best shot: "Mary," she said, "you can't fight the cells that are killing your daughter, but you can take all that frustration and do something useful with it. You can go out and tell people, 'I need your help! Others need your help!' Then even if Anissa dies you'll know in your heart that you did every last thing you could to save her. And, Mary, others will live because of what you did."

Then a remarkable thing happened. As Tami describes it, "This weepy, devastated little lady got up out of her chair and stood there, 12 feet tall, and said, 'Tell me exactly what to do because I'm going to do it.' "

So began the Ayalas' long odyssey in search of the stranger who could save Anissa's life. Because bone marrow controls the immune system, whose countless thousands of cellular interactions determine when people get sick and whether they recover, the match they needed had to be closer than one for a heart, liver or lung transplant.

Although the registry coordinating center in Minneapolis found no potential donor matches for Anissa, the family pushed tenaciously ahead. After nine days of evaluation and treatment, Anissa was sent home from Children's Hospital. Doctors there recommended that her therapy be continued at a cancer center specializing in bone-marrow transplantation (BMT) for adults. So the Ayalas began canvassing other hospitals, and found the one they were looking for ten miles from home. It was called City of Hope.

Only two years had passed since bone marrow from an unrelated donor was first successfully transplanted to a leukemia patient at the sprawling complex in the shadow of the San Gabriel Mountains. But the City of Hope National Medical Center had already taken its place among the handful of American hospitals pioneering what was then a last-chance procedure fraught with unknowns.

To Anissa, driving across the grounds with her parents on a spring morning, it seemed more like a college campus than a hospital, with its clusters of palm trees and flowering shrubs highlighting neatly clipped lawns.

The pediatric oncologist at City of Hope took Anissa off the chemotherapy pills and put her on interferon, an experimental drug at the time, which was intended to stave off the acute phase of her leukemia. Anissa had to inject herself with it every day. The shot left her feeling feverish and achy, as though she had the flu, but her white and red blood cells began to come back into balance. Her other symptoms disappeared as well.

Meanwhile, Anissa's fight had become her family's fight. There was rarely a night when one or more of the Ayalas, even shy Airon, and sometimes all four, were not out somewhere, at a service-club meeting or a school rally, describing the shadow over Anissa's life and how it darkened with every passing day.

Assisted by Life-Savers, the Ayalas went out armed with data and heartbreaking case histories detailing the critical need for marrow donors, particularly from ethnic minorities. They handed out addresses of neighborhood blood-collection centers, and they offered reassurances that the initial test was simply a matter of giving a little blood. And Anissa, discovering skills as a spokesperson not only for herself but also for a cause, told mesmerized listeners, "I'm dying. Would you help me if you could? Well, you might be able to." Or, "In this audience, right now, there is someone who can save a life. Maybe not mine, but somebody's!"

"She astonished me," said Tami Brown. In those early months when Life-Savers began directing the search for a donor, she looked at Anissa and saw a stylishly dressed teen-ager with a great smile whose parents doted on her and hardly ever said no to her. Tami wondered if she was tough enough to stand up under the weight of her terrible affliction.

"I soon found out that there was more to this young lady than a trendy outfit and matching earrings. She was made of tough stuff. Fighting against odds that might have paralyzed a more mature person, she didn't buckle. She battled back."

And so did her family. As the Ayalas took their story out into the community, people began to sign up to be tissue-typed; first a few, then a few dozen. Then by the hundreds and the thousands.

Airon Ayala: Everything became second to the telephone calls and the drives and the rallies. Dad belonged to the Lions Club and the Elks Lodge, and Mom belonged to the

Walnut Junior Women's Club, and all of them handed out our fliers and invited us to speak. They collected thousands of dollars for our cause.

We became experts in the field and could rattle off the statistics and the terminology as if we'd all been to medical school. We went into neighboring communities. The local press and TV did little stories about us. Then the kids at Walnut High School started knocking on doors, and on three consecutive Saturdays they got 1500 people tissue-typed and raised more than $40,000 to help pay for the tests.

I keep saying "we." I did the least. My dad was the smartest planner, my mother the hardest worker and Anissa the best speaker. Mostly I just tagged along. Public speaking was not my thing. But whenever I did speak, I always said the same thing: my sister was the bravest person I knew, and she deserved to live.

Maybe it was an idea whose time had come. But the fact is that in those 20 months that the Ayalas—and other afflicted families—were roused to heighten public interest in their cause, the national registry of potential marrow donors leapt from 17,000 names to 157,079 (it now stands at almost three million), and the number of transplants performed rose from a bare handful to 533 a year.

But Anissa was not one of them.

The weeks and months marched by, and though by now her name was on registers in Canada and England, the telephone call the Ayalas prayed for didn't come. Anissa continued to project remarkable optimism by day, but she began to be plagued by nightmares and would come dragging her blankets into her parents' bedroom.

Then a year and a half into the desperate search, the call did come, excitedly reporting that a donor match for Anissa had been found. They would be in touch when all the details were pinned down.

The joy in the Ayala household was beyond belief. But when days passed with no further word, anxiety closed in on them again. Tami Brown found out the devastating truth: someone had jumped the gun. There had been a potential donor, but at the last minute he or she had backed out.

Stunned, Mary, Abe and Airon retreated into dazed silence. But a transcendent calm came over Anissa. "This all has to be part of God's plan," she said. "I believe he is not going to let it end this way."

Deep down, her mother and father felt the same way. They had taken the first step on a long, gallant and incredibly difficult passage whose outcome could not be predicted.

Mary: Bobbie Roger, Dr. Gutierrez's sister, was one of the dear friends who ago-nized through that whole hard time with us. Like us, she counted the passing days, know-ing that while we might still come up with a donor, the odds against it were building. In the meantime those sick white cells in Anissa could become killers at any time. Near the end of the year, when Bobbie asked me what I was going to do, I started listing the meet-ings and rallies we had scheduled.

She interrupted. "You're running out of time, Mary."

"Well, what else can I do?"

"You can have a baby."

I flinched. I wasn't even sure she was serious. "Give me a break," I answered. "I'm 41 years old and my husband has had a vasectomy. Do you believe in miracles?"

But she wouldn't back off. "Vasectomies can be reversed. And let's face it, you've run out of options."

I told her it would never work; it was a wild idea. But even as I was arguing, her idea was making its way into my heart. The truth is I'd always wanted another child, but I knew Abe considered our family complete.

Sure enough, when I tried it out on him he said I was crazy—half our friends were already grandparents—and I again tried to forget it. But I kept hearing Bobbie's voice: "You've run out of options." I remembered Tami Brown telling me that I needed to know in my heart that I'd done everything possible to save my daughter; I longed for that peace of mind. Whatever happened I had to know that we had done everything in our power to keep Anissa from dying.

And yet there were questions that tore at me. By now I well knew what a bone-marrow aspiration was; I had seen them insert those needles into Anissa's hips. Could we subject an infant to such a procedure? And how could I go against Abe's resistance to the very idea of our having another baby?

I met with a minister and asked him how I could be sure of what God expected of me. He said I must search my heart, that God would let me know. But late at night, when I lay in the dark of the silent house and searched my heart, I heard two voices. One said, "Yes, do it." The other said, "No, it's not right."

Abe and I talked about it endlessly. He just didn't think it would work, and he couldn't bear the thought of seeing Anissa crushed again by another false hope. Neither could I, but what other chance did we have?

He said, "We might still find a match." But I knew he didn't really believe it.

I spoke with a doctor who assured me there would be minimal risk to the baby beyond a little soreness around the hips for an hour or so afterward. In about a week, the marrow would completely regenerate.

When I told this to Abe he didn't speak for a while. Then I realized that his eyes had suddenly gone misty. "What?" I asked.

"I was just thinking that even if she ... even if we lost her, another kid in the house would help us bear it."

We clung to each other. We talked and prayed. But we were still paralyzed by our fears and doubts. One day it was yes, the next day no.

Researching our chances of success, we came to realize just how awesome the odds against us were. Under the best circumstances, there is only a 50-50 chance that a man who has undergone a reverse vasectomy will impregnate his partner. As for me, I had reached an age bracket in which a woman's chances of conceiving decline dramatically. Even then, there is only a 25-percent chance any two siblings will have compatible bone-marrow antigens. And finally, cruelly, even with a related donor, up to 40 percent of transplant recipients die within two years of the operation.

Later that same week, I woke up before dawn with my heart pounding and shook Abe awake. Breathlessly I told him I had had a dream that seemed to be saying I should go ahead and have a baby, that everything would work out. "I think I finally know what God wants of us, Abe," I said.

We were sitting up in the bed. Abe put his arm around me. "Listen, I want you to go *see Dr. Gutierrez today,"* he said. *"Make sure you're okay to get pregnant."* He took a deep breath. *"Then find out what a guy who's had a vasectomy does when he changes his mind."*

Now the quest turned in this new direction: an audacious gamble against almost invincible odds. Once Mary and Abe made the decision, they realized it was inevitable. What parent, they would ask, face to face with the death of a beloved child, would not have done this?

That day Mary turned up at Dr. Gutierrez's and asked, "Am I crazy? Am I too old?"

The doctor hugged her. "I'm going to examine you, but from what I know, I don't think you're too old." Mary got an unqualified go-ahead.

Typically, the way was rocky. Even after Abe underwent the surgery that reversed his vasectomy, his sperm count was anemic. "Don't get your hopes up," said the urologist.

By then it was March 1989. Four more months passed, and nothing happened to challenge the doctor's pessimism. Then in July tests came back that once more sent the Ayalas' hopes soaring. Mary was pregnant.

"I was ecstatic," she says. "I don't think any of us could separate our feelings—the joy of having a baby in the family and the new hope we could now hold out for Anissa—but we felt more than doubly blessed. We felt the hand of God."

But those feelings were overlaid with anxieties every day. Would Anissa remain in remission long enough for the baby to be born and grow old enough to undergo a marrow aspiration? And would the baby's marrow even match? There was still no way to know any of the answers. And so the family never stopped searching registries for a nonrelated donor.

In November, when Mary entered the fourth month of her pregnancy, her obstetrician suggested that she undergo amniocentesis, which is routinely performed on expectant mothers past the age of 35. In this procedure amniotic fluid is drawn from the sac surrounding the fetus and tested for genetic abnormalities. It also reveals the sex of the fetus.

At first Mary said no. She and Abe had already discussed it and decided that this child was going to be theirs to keep and love no matter what impairment he or she might be born with.

"Also," says Mary, "I absolutely did not want to know if the baby was a match, or a boy or a girl; I didn't want any conflicting feelings. I just wanted to have a normal, joyful pregnancy."

But when Mary and Abe were told some potential health problems could be corrected in the womb, they decided to have the test. After it was scheduled they learned of an additional benefit: a City of Hope doctor described a promising new procedure in which the umbilical-cord blood, rich in the stem cells from which all blood cells develop, is frozen at birth and used in a transplant with the donor marrow. But before doing this, doctors could find out through amniocentesis if the baby's antigens matched Anissa's.

Mary: Four weeks passed before we heard anything. Then the clinic called and said they had some results: the baby was a girl, and she was perfectly healthy.

"Thank you," I whispered. We were all in the kitchen. Abe, Airon and Anissa immediately knew from my voice what it was about, and they were all staring at me. I told them the news and in half a second we were all crying. Finally I asked, "Is there anything about the antigen match?"

"Not yet."

Now that the answer to the last crucial question was imminent, every waiting day seemed an eternity. Christmas came and went, then it was 1990. All of January passed, and still we received no news.

We kept busy with our marrow-donor drives and kept talking to civic groups, but mostly we waited. We occupied ourselves thinking of a name for our baby, but that came to us quickly enough: Marissa Eve, combining my name with Anissa's, and invoking the blessing of the first Eve—giver of life. After that we never talked about "the baby," only Marissa.

On February 16, a Friday, I was in Abe's little office above the shop preparing the payroll when the doctor called. "Mary!" she sang out. "We have a match!"

"What?"

"We have a match!"

*I couldn't speak. I could barely breathe. Then I yelled over the intercom, "Abe! Abe!"
He came running up the stairs, scared, calling, "What? What's the matter?" And I flew
into his arms, overjoyed.*

For Anissa, who had dropped out of school for a time, the news
brought fresh strength. Doctors told her that if Marissa was an average
size, they might be able to do the aspiration when the infant was six
months old.

The way ahead would be beset with new, unforeseen haz-
ards. When a local reporter telephoned to ask what was new,
Anissa told her that her mother was pregnant, and that the
Ayalas hoped the baby would be a match. No one in the family considered it a secret.

Next day the story was on page one of the San Gabriel
Valley *Tribune.* Then the Los Angeles *Times* picked up the story
and gave it an "ethical" slant: "It is extremely rare for a baby
to be conceived specifically to serve as a bone-marrow donor
for an ailing family member. Unlike adults, children are unable
to give informed consent for such medical procedures."

The Ayalas were appalled, not only that so private a matter should suddenly become widespread public property, but
also that their painstakingly considered and intensely felt decision should now be subject to the casual judgment of
strangers. They declined all media requests for interviews, hoping the
controversy would subside.

But it didn't. No one, it seemed, was without a fiercely held opinion.
Self-appointed guardians of moral correctness took to the press to
denounce "this strip mining of babies' bodies," causing the taking of
marrow under anesthetic to sound like an amputation. Stunned by the

onslaught, already under terrific stress, Mary was often driven to tears by the attacks. Retreating to a corner of the house, alone with her conscience, she would pray for sustenance.

One day Abe said that the way the story was coming out was detrimental to the whole national effort to recruit potential marrow donors. "We have to tell our side of it," he said. Soon the Ayalas were being profiled in newspaper articles and on television, even becoming the subject of a *Time* magazine cover story. They corrected a basic misconception about marrow transplants by explaining there were no body "parts" involved.

Some medical ethicists rose to their defense. Arthur Caplan, now director of The Center for Bioethics at the University of Pennsylvania Health System, pointed out that people often have babies without even thinking about the why of it, and that many children are called to life, at least in part, by adult desires to experience parenthood, to provide an heir or, as happened in the past, to have another pair of hands on the farm. "In this case a child is being born at least partly from a notion of humanity," Caplan said.

Dr. Norman Fost, a pediatrician and ethicist at the University of Wisconsin School of Medicine, agreed: "Of all the reasons people have children, I think this is one of the better ones: to save a life."

Perhaps the best judges were those who had walked in the Ayalas' shoes. Wrote such a mother and father to the Los Angeles *Times:* "As parents of a 16-year-old son who died of leukemia, we rejoice for the Ayala family. We wish conceiving one child to save another had been an option for us 26 years ago. How can there be controversy over the addition of the miracle baby to this family?"

Abe: Marissa was due around April 15. On a Tuesday evening two weeks before, Mary and I were getting ready to go to our Lamaze birth preparation class when her water broke. We all panicked a little. We had been given specific instructions that as soon as she went into labor, we were to call not only the obstetrician but also all the people at City of Hope who would be collecting the umbilical-cord blood. They all had to get over to Citrus Valley Medical Center—Queen of the Valley Campus along with all their gear. But nobody was prepared for April 3.

At Queen of the Valley, the obstetrician said Mary wasn't ready to deliver, but he didn't want to risk infection by sending her home. By now the doctors from City of Hope were arriving. There were huddled consultations, then the recommendation: a Caesarean section. Mary, sitting in a wheelchair, clutched my hand and asked, "Can Abe be there?" They said yes, and they wheeled her toward the operating room. I went trotting after them.

I wasn't sure I could handle it, but I knew I had to stay close to Mary, for both our sakes. They put one of those green gowns and a mask on me and I tried to stay out of the way. We were a crowd: the obstetrician and two obstetrical nurses, Marissa's pediatrician, and the doctors and nurses there to collect and freeze the umbilical-cord blood.

It didn't take long. Mary had had a general anesthetic, so I was the first in the family to see Marissa. The nurses had cleaned her up and weighed her. Then they showed her to me: a six-pound, four-ounce beauty, 18 inches long, with dark brown hair and eyes. When Mary came around and they put Marissa in her arms, we thanked God together.

Marissa brought unqualified joy to the Ayala family. They all felt a new spirit, a surge of hope, when Mary carried her through the door. Within a few days it was hard for them to imagine what life in their house had been like before she came to them. "One of us was always cuddling and kissing her," says Airon, "or making up some excuse to go into her room when she was asleep, just to look at her."

For Anissa, it was as though the newborn baby had already demonstrated healing powers. She had dropped out of school to spend more time recruiting donors, so she spent long stretches by herself studying. There were times when her fears could not be held in check. During those moments, she would often go and sit by Marissa's crib and contentedly read, or watch the sleeping child. A great calm would descend on her.

It had been two years since Anissa's leukemia was diagnosed, and she knew her time was running out. Each new day stepped up the likelihood that the sick white cells in her marrow would regain the upper hand.

Sometimes Anissa would look at the sleeping infant and wonder whether that had been the limit of God's plan, to bring them this precious child to fill an empty place in the house. Marissa, perfect, beautiful, was petite like her mother, and the doctors wanted her to grow bigger before they performed the transplant. Anissa could only wait.

In the meantime the teen-ager had her family's support, her own resilient spirit and another ally fate brought her way. One warm August day, Mary and Abe were getting ready to go to a swim party at the home of their friends Glenda and Fernando Espinosa. They asked Anissa to join them. First she said no, she didn't think so. But then she called out, "Wait a minute, I changed my mind."

It was a snap decision, an impulse. But it was like a railroad switch that sent her down a new track, toward somebody with whom she could share everything, including the vulnerability she tried to hide from her family.

His name was Bryan Espinosa.

Although their parents were close friends, he and Anissa had never met. Bryan had graduated from Walnut High School five years before her. But now when they were introduced, the response was instantaneous. Bryan was barbecuing, and after they'd exchanged a few words Anissa became his helper. She found out he had just started his own company, an office janitorial service, and that he had a wonderful sense of humor. Best of all, he was not in the least intimidated by her disease.

Other boys either tried to pretend there was nothing the matter with Anissa or acted as though she were breakable. That was not Bryan's way. He had her laughing all day, while beneath the jokes he showed consideration and concern.

Bryan remembers hearing about Anissa long before they met. "My folks talked about her all the time; somehow I felt I already knew her." That day he took one look at her and felt they were meant to be.

In the joyful spirit of the day, Bryan's father threw Anissa, fully dressed, into the swimming pool. Bryan lent her a sweat suit to change into. Before she went home, there had been no word between them about getting together again, so she planned to wash and iron the sweat suit, then telephone Bryan to arrange its return.

But he beat her to it. Mary called her to the phone the next morning with a knowing smile: "It's Bryan."

"Hi," he said. "You forgot your sister's pacifier."

"Well, how come you didn't just tell my mother?" she teased.

"Guess," he said, adding that he had a good video movie, *Driving Miss Daisy.* Did she want to see it? She said yes. That afternoon he brought it around. Then they went to have pizza. By the time he went home that night they both knew that whatever the future might bring, whatever there was of it, they were going to share it.

Bryan never dated another girl after that, and six months later—February 14, St. Valentine's Day, 1991—they became engaged.

This new turn in Anissa's life and Bryan's persistent support were critical. On May 22 the three-year quest for a cure came to an end. On that date Marissa's doctor decided that the little girl, now 14 months old and weighing 16 pounds, was ready for the aspiration. Anissa was admitted to City of Hope for a series of tests and to be prepared for her transplant.

When word leaked out, a media battalion laid siege to the hospital: TV vans with their snaking wires and satellite dishes and journalists from all over the United States. The hospital issued only a brief statement. The family said nothing.

Security guards were stationed outside Anissa's door around the clock. Within the week she received a four-hour infusion of high-dose chemotherapy and the first of 11 treatments of full-body radiation. Her blood count plummeted. The treatment was intended to completely destroy her cancerous bone marrow. It left her frail, bald and suffering from nausea, vomiting and ulcerating mouth sores. Because she was unable to tolerate food, Anissa was fed intravenously.

It also wiped out her immune system, leaving her without any defense against infection. For the next three weeks, she was kept in total isolation, confined to a room with specially filtered air, into which family and close friends could be admitted only after washing thoroughly and putting on surgical gowns, sterile caps and masks.

"It was a heartbreaking thing," said Mary. "A week before, she'd been a vibrant, healthy-looking young girl, and because of a decision we made, she had been brought to the edge of death. You couldn't help thinking: Did we do the right thing? Would it have been better to leave her in peace with what little time she had left?"

With the new flood of newspaper stories and TV coverage came another spate of abusive letters. Mary and Abe were terrified by a rumor that critics might file an injunction blocking Marissa's participation because she was incapable of giving permission.

Abe: For Mary and me, this threat at the decisive hour was almost more than we could bear. We saw Anissa alone, at the very end of a lifeline, and feared people were trying to cut it.

Not sure what might happen, we didn't take Marissa out of the house during that entire last week. Then, before dawn on June 4, we brought her to City of Hope. By pre-arrangement, we entered through a back way far from the main entrance. Anissa was in oncology, another building, and though Mary and I agonized about it, there was never any real question about where we had to be. Anissa at least knew what was happening to her and that we would be close by.

By 8 a.m., the doctors put Marissa to sleep with a general anesthetic. The hard part was knowing they were inserting those inch-long needles into each hip. We realized she was sound asleep and felt nothing; we had been assured that not one donor in the whole history of marrow transplantation had ever suffered a serious reaction. But neither of us could breathe easily until it was over.

In 30 minutes it was done, and the marrow, supplemented by cells extracted from Marissa's umbilical cord, was on its way to the oncology wing. We wanted to go there immediately, but how could we leave until we saw Marissa awake and alert and herself again?

At midmorning those gleaming brown eyes suddenly opened and looked straight at us. Marissa grinned, the way she always did when she first saw us in the morning, and would have jumped right out of bed if we hadn't coaxed her down. By noon she was scampering down the hospital corridor as though she had just wakened from a nap. So Bryan's mother, whose face and car were unfamiliar even to the local journalists, slipped her past the press and took her home.

Then Mary and I rushed to oncology to be with Anissa.

Airon and Bryan had been waiting outside Anissa's room for hours. Until a nurse drew the curtain across the big glass window, they could see her smiling at them bravely. She noticed the big red balloons they held that said "Happy Birthday." It wasn't her birthday, but she knew what they meant: the start of her new life.

When the marrow arrived, it was injected into Anissa by a catheter through an incision in her chest. The dark red, life-giving marrow flowed into her bloodstream. There the cells began finding their way to her bone cavities.

"She was barely alive," remembers Abe. "She looked as though a breeze would blow her away."

Still, they were all on a kind of high at first, knowing it was done and Anissa was alive. But as the days passed, she showed no signs of gaining strength. No one could say whether the transplant would take, and they had to hide their anxiety when they came to visit.

They all knew too much about the potential for trouble down the road to have any real peace of mind. There was always the possibility of infection and of transplant-related pneumonia. And there was not only medicine's eternal challenge of the body rejecting the foreign tissue, but also the opposite chance that the new cells would launch an antibody attack on the patient—the primary cause of most marrow-transplant failures.

Through these anxious times Bryan was best at keeping Anissa's spirits up. He came early in the morning and stayed until they made him leave, often near midnight. He was intensely protective of her; he knew that if anyone walked into that room with so much as a cold she was dead, so he double-checked every visitor. The nurses dubbed him "Dr. Bryan."

He also made Anissa laugh and lightened her days. He brought her a sporty white cap to cover her bald head and teased that she was the prettiest boy he'd ever seen. When her white blood cell count started back up he cheered; when it crashed, he consoled, "That's still more than you had when you started."

Mary and Abe tried to match Bryan's sunny outlook, but they kept remembering how their daughter had to build an entirely new immune system from the comparatively small number of cells that Marissa had given her. And even that didn't show up right away. Finally her white cell count stood at 100.

The doctor had said that when the count went to 1000—the first sign that Marissa's cells were grafting and multiplying—she could come out of isolation, so Abe put a calendar up on the wall and they kept track, day by day—200, 300. Then it crashed back down to 100. The next day it was up to 800—but then came another crash.

Marissa was not allowed into her room, but Mary and Abe often brought the baby around to the little Japanese garden outside her sister's window so they could wave to each other and Anissa could watch her play. That gave her strength too. She told her mother, "I have to be here to see her grow up."

Finally, three weeks after the transplant, Anissa's white cell count pushed over 1000, and kept climbing, and she was allowed to leave the room where she had been cloistered. She was still very weak and had bad days. But color had come back to her cheeks, and she was eating regular food. She was past the first hurdle.

A week later, on July 5, a statement by her doctor was given to the press: Anissa had been discharged. Her recovery had been "excellent," he wrote, but infection, rejection and recurrence of the leukemia all remained threats in the coming days, and he would say nothing about her long-term prognosis.

That same day Anissa came home. She was greeted by a crowd of family and friends who cheered and waved banners and balloons to welcome her back. Under the brim of the bright red hat she wore, her eyes were swimming with tears. She blew kisses and hugged Marissa and Airon extra hard.

Mary had made Anissa's bedroom as sterile as she could get it. She scrubbed the floors and windows, and on the door to the room posted a hand-lettered sign: "Germs Stay Out!"

During the weeks Anissa spent there, Marissa was her constant companion, playing quietly on the floor, chattering, brushing and rebrushing the stubble of hair freshly sprouting on Anissa's head.

The little girl helped her sister pass the time until she'd reached the milestone of 100 days without complications. Then Anissa could experience simple pleasures that had been denied her: going outdoors without a mask, eating fruits and vegetables that hadn't been allowed. But most important, the Ayalas could feel like a normal family again. As Anissa recovered her strength, she and her mother focused on one important task: planning the wedding.

One year and one day after the transplant—on June 5, 1992—Anissa and Bryan were married. It was one of those dazzling California evenings filled with promise: a lingering red sunset, a softly darkening sky lit with countless stars. In ways large and small, virtually every one of the 350 guests— doctors, nurses, marrow-donor caseworkers or simply people who prayed for her—had played some role in her recovery. They were all there to celebrate the miracle of her new life.

Anissa came down the aisle, beautiful as every bride is, on the arm of her proud father. Preceding them, glowing with pride and bearing her sister's wedding ring on a small cushion, was two-year-old Marissa. Mary looked at her two daughters and breathed a silent thanks for what was there before her: two wonderful daughters who, together, made a miracle happen.

ACKNOWLEDGMENTS

All the stories in *The Power of Healing* previously appeared in Reader's Digest magazine. We would like to thank the following contributors and publishers for permission to reprint material.

"I See the Mailbox" by Susan E. Bischoff. © 1994 by Susan E. Bischoff. Sarasota Herald-Tribune (October 16, '94).

The Daddy Prize by Robert Fulghum. "IT WAS ON FIRE WHEN I LAY DOWN ON IT," copyright © 1988, 1989 by Robert Fulghum. Reprinted by permission of Villard Books, a division of Random House, Inc.

Christmas Lost and Found by Shirley Barksdale. © 1988 by Shirley Barksdale. McCall's (December '88).

Helping Friends Who Grieve by Lois Duncan. © 1990 by Lois Duncan. Woman's Day (October 2, '90).

Doc Tenney's Healing Magic by Allen M. Schoen and Pam Proctor. "LOVE, MIRACLES AND ANIMAL HEALING," copyright © 1995 by Allen M. Schoen, DVM, MS, and Pam Proctor. Reprinted with the permission of Simon & Schuster.

Finding My Way With Jesse by Scott Russell Sanders. "HUNTING FOR HOPE," copyright © 1996 by Scott Russell Sanders. Published by Beacon Press. This material also appeared in Orion Magazine.

Reunion of Two Hearts by Edie Clark. © 1995 by Yankee Publishing Inc. Yankee (May '95).

Family Ties by Linda Ching Sledge. © 1999 by by Linda Ching Sledge. Parenting (November '99).

Quotations:

Ursula K. LeGuin, "THE LATHE OF HEAVEN," (Scribner).
Doug Larson, United Feature Syndicate.
Nikki Giovanni, "BLACK FEELING, BLACK TALK, BLACK JUDG-MENT," (William Morrow).
Anne Frank, "THE DIARY OF A YOUNG GIRL," (Doubleday).
Ruth E. Renkel in Bourbon, Indiana, News-Mirror (February 2, '94).
Charlotte Scholl in True Story (December '64).
Henry Boye in National Enquirer (August 27, '96).

Biblical scriptures are from the "REVISED STANDARD VERSION OF THE BIBLE," National Council of the Churches of Christ in the USA (Thomas Nelson).

PHOTO CREDITS

Cover hands photo by Michael Ziegler/age fotostock

Cover wheat field photo by Steve Gravano/age fotostock

p. 5:   Anne Shamel/Graphistock

p. 10:   Ann Cutting/photonica

p. 15:   Matthew Benson/Tony Stone Worldwide

p. 18:   Index Stock Photography

p. 26:   Vera Storman/Tony Stone Worldwide

p. 30:   Peter Davidian/photonica

p. 35:   Jayne Hinds Bidaut/Graphistock

p. 38:   Gunther/Photo Researchers, Inc.

p. 42:   Garry D. McMichael/Photo Researchers, Inc.

p. 47:   Kent and Donna Dannen/Photo Researchers, Inc.

p. 51:   A. Ramey/PhotoEdit

p. 59:   Doug Plummer/photonica

p. 60:   Andy Levin/Photo Researchers, Inc.

p. 64:   Sherrie Hunt/Graphistock

p. 70:   Lisa Spindler/Graphistock

p. 74:   Ken Sherman/Graphistock

p. 76-77: Andre Baranowski/Graphistock

p. 79:   Barnaby Hall/photonica

p. 83: Index Stock Photography

p. 86: David Muench/Tony Stone Worldwide

p. 88-89: Leslye Borden/PhotoEdit

p. 91: Gary A. Conner/PhotoEdit

p. 94-95: Leo de Wys/Stock Photo Agency

p. 96: Bruce Ayres/Tony Stone Worldwide

p. 97: Bill Cardoni/Tony Stone Worldwide

p. 98-99: Jack Dykinga/Tony Stone Worldwide

p. 100: Chris Ferebee/Graphistock

p. 105: Darrell Gulin/Tony Stone Worldwide

p. 108: William Meyer/Index Stock Imagery

p. 110: Joshua Sheldon/photonica

p. 118-119: Paul Clancy/Graphistock

p. 121: Myrleen Ferguson/PhotoEdit

p. 124-125: Gail Mooney/Corbis

p. 128: Joseph Nettis/Photo Researchers, Inc.

p. 133: Luciana Frigerio/Graphistock

p. 135: Index Stock Imagery

p. 136-137: The Picture Book/photonica

p. 141: Vera Storman/Tony Stone Worldwide

p. 144: Lisa Spindler/Graphistock

p. 148: Jean-Paul Thomas-Jacana/Photo Researchers, Inc.

p. 153: Herbert Schwind/Okapia/Photo Researchers, Inc.

p. 154-155: Rod Planck/Photo Researchers, Inc.

p. 156: David Young-Wolf/PhotoEdit

p. 161: Index Stock Imagery

p. 164: Index Stock Imagery

p. 166: Anthony Mercieca/Photo Researchers, Inc.

p. 171: Leigh Beisch/Graphistock

p. 179: Scala/Art Resource

p. 183: Deborah Davis/Tony Stone Worldwide